HEKATE LIMINAL RITES

"Then, earth began to bellow, trees to dance
And howling dogs in glimmering light advance
Ere Hecate came."

THE AENEID, VIRGIL, LATE C1ST BCE, TRANS. J. DRYDEN.

OTHER BOOKS BY THESE AUTHORS

By Sorita d'Este & David Rankine
THE ISLES OF THE MANY GODS
VISIONS OF THE CAILLEACH
THE GUISES OF THE MORRIGAN
PRACTICAL ELEMENTAL MAGICK
PRACTICAL PLANETARY MAGICK
CIRCLE OF FIRE
WICCA MAGICKAL BEGINNINGS

By Sorita d'Este
ARTEMIS – VIRGIN GODDESS OF THE SUN & MOON
TOWARDS THE WICCAN CIRCLE
HEKATE KEYS TO THE CROSSROADS (EDITOR)
PRIESTESSES PYTHONESSES & SIBYLS (EDITOR)
HORNS OF POWER (EDITOR)
BOTH SIDES OF HEAVEN (EDITOR)

By David Rankine
BECOMING MAGICK
CLIMBING THE TREE OF LIFE
CRYSTALS HEALING & FOLKLORE
HEKA ANCIENT EGYPTIAN MAGIC & RITUAL

By David Rankine, with Stephen Skinner
A COLLECTION OF MAGICAL SECRETS
PRACTICAL ANGEL MAGIC OF DR JOHN DEE'S ENOCHIAN TABLES
KEYS TO THE GATEWAY OF MAGIC
THE GOETIA OF DR RUDD
THE VERITABLE KEY OF SOLOMON

Published by Avalonia

BM Avalonia
London
WC1N 3XX
England, UK

www.avaloniabooks.co.uk

HEKATE LIMINAL RITES
Copyright © Sorita and David Rankine 2009

ISBN-10: 1905297238
ISBN-13: 978-1905297238

First Edition, May 2009
Design by Satori

Cover art "Hecate" by Joanna Barnum

COVER IMAGE "HECATE" BY JOANNA BARNUM

FOR MORE INFORMATION ON THIS ARTIST, VISIT HER WEBSITE:
WWW.JOANNABARNUM.COM

DEDICATED TO ANDREW COLLINS
WHO KNOWS **ALL** ABOUT LIMINAL RITES!

HEKATE
LIMINAL RITES

A STUDY OF THE RITUALS, MAGIC AND SYMBOLS OF THE
TORCH-BEARING TRIPLE GODDESS OF THE CROSSROADS

SORITA D'ESTE AND DAVID RANKINE

PUBLISHED BY AVALONIA 2009

Acknowledgements

We would like to extend a special thank you to:

Stephen Ronan, for his kind permission to use his translations of Proclus *Hymn to Hekate and Janus* and the *Prayer to Selene for Any Operation* as previously published in his own excellent work *The Goddess Hekate*.

Zachary Yardley for the use of his previously unpublished renditions of a number of the ancient texts reproduced in this volume.

Joanna Barnum, for permission to use the awesome image of the Goddess Hekate which graces the cover of this book, available from www.joannabarnum.com

Vitoria Laurel, for her encouragement and support in our work.

Alan O'Flynn for permission to use his photograph of Hekate from the temple at Lagina.

Dave Surber from wildwinds.com for permission to reproduce the images in the chapter *Coins*.

To everyone who enjoyed *Hekate Keys to the Crossroads* and told us so,

May you all prosper in all that you desire and may the flame of kinship burn as a beacon forever more.

The Keybearers will always find each other.

CONTENTS

Acknowledgements *8*

A Note on Terminology *12*

A Note on Her Name *13*

Foreword **14**

From the Three-Ways **19**

Literary Sources *31*

In Her Service **37**

Hesiod *37*

Empedocles *38*

Porphyry *39*

Circe *41*

Medea *42*

The Witches of Thessaly *44*

Lampads *45*

Hekate's Vegetarian Followers *46*

Sacred Eleusis **48**

Images of Hekate **58**

Voces Magicae **65**

Charms from the PGM **70**

List of Charms in the Greek Magical Papyri *71*

Symbols from the PGM *74*

Bear Charm *75*

Charm of Hekate Ereschigal *76*

Charms for Love **78**

Defixiones **84**

The Armour of Hekate **89**

Glimpses of Initiation **91**

Herbs & Poisons.. **94**
   Aconite *95*
   Ebony.. *95*
   Garlic... *96*
   Mandrake... *96*
   Oak *97*
   Saffron *98*
   Yew... *98*
   Unspecified Herbs... *99*
   Herb Gathering *100*

Sacred Bronze **102**

Iron Nails & Rings.. **105**

Hekate & The Angels **107**

Coins.. **110**

From Sleep **114**

Oracles of Hekate **117**

Offerings **120**

Hekate Suppers **126**

Invocation.. **129**

Hymns.. **132**
   Proclus Hymn to Hekate and Janus *132*
   Prayer to Selene for any operation........................... *133*

Animal Formed.. **137**
   Cow-Headed/Bull-Headed *137*
   Dog-Headed *139*
   Dragon-Headed... *139*
   Goat-Headed.. *140*
   Horse-Headed... *140*
   Serpent-Headed *141*

Necromancy & Reanimation............................ **143**

Death Magic **149**

Underworld...................................... **151**

Black Dogs.. **154**

Serpents **157**

The Strophalos **159**

King Solomon................................... **163**

Fusions **169**
    Artemis-Hekate *169*
    Bendis.. *170*
    Bona Dea *171*
    Brimo.. *171*
    Despoina *172*
    Ereschigal-Hekate..................................... *172*
    Isis-Hekate *173*
    Physis *174*
    Selene-Hekate... *175*

Bibliography **177**

Index... **189**

MEDEA PREPARING MAGIC POTION OF REANIMATION, FROM KRAUSS 1690

A Note on Terminology

We need at this point to clarify terminology used in this work. *Daimon* (*individual destiny*) is a Greek word and distinct from the derivative word demon. A daimon was a supernatural being lower than the gods but higher than man, such as a demi-god or the ghost of a dead hero. Plato and his pupil Xenocrates categorised daimones as good or bad, the former being known as *eudaemons* and the latter as *kakodaemons*. Prior to this daimon was a much more general term, sometimes even being used to describe gods. Distinct from this usage *demon* is the Christian term specifically relating to a negative (in their theology) supernatural being.

A Note on Her Name

As you might expect with a liminal goddess like Hekate, the moment you start looking into the details around her, you find variations and different possibilities. Even the meaning of her name, *Hekate*, is uncertain. The most popular translation of her name is from the word *Hekatos*, meaning '*worker from afar*', though *Hekaton*, meaning '*a hundred*', has also been suggested.

"You, O Hecate,
Who know untold desires that work our will
And art the mistress of our secret spells."

Metamorphoses, Ovid, 8CE, trans. H. Gregory.

FOREWORD

Hekate stands at the crossroads bearing the keys to the mysteries. In the ancient world she inspired poets and philosophers, witches, magicians and ordinary people, all of whom knew she could bestow blessings to improve their lot and protect them from the harsh denizens of the infernal realm. Today she continues to inspire and evoke awe in those who encounter her; for some in subtle ways, leading them in an elusive nameless manner with her symbols, for others in a more powerful and directly empowering way.

There are still people today whom Hekate continues to call to her mysteries – encouraging them to reach into the innermost parts of their souls to find the power that illuminates the darkness. We have been fortunate to encounter some of these individuals over the years, they come from all walks of life and from all over the world. Men and women who continue to explore her mysteries through practices such as magic, witchcraft, herbalism and through song, art and dance. Amongst them modern day witches and magicians, shamans and mystics, each seeking to understand the arcane power that she continues to radiate.

In 2005 Sorita edited the anthology *Hekate: Keys to the Crossroads*, which gathered together experiential essays from more than twenty people writing about their work with and personal understanding of Hekate. It was clear from the contributions that the goddess Hekate is still alive and well within the hearts and minds of an informal modern priesthood today. She had definitely not been consigned to the obscurity of the *'forgotten gods'*.

In order to gain a better understanding of her placement within the pantheons of the Ancient World, we have been researching her for a number of years. During this time we have looked at a diverse range of evidence left behind by those who honoured her, were inspired by her or had a fascination with her throughout history. We found clues and evidence relating to Hekate in sources stretching back more than three thousand years into and beyond the Greek Dark Ages.

On many occasions whilst we were pursuing a line of inquiry for one of our other projects, we encountered references to Hekate. Sometimes these were in unexpected places, resulting in a number of tangential studies to discover facets of this goddess that we had not previously come across in works dedicated to her.

This book *Hekate Liminal Rites* is part of a long term research project we are working on. In it we have brought together a collection of material which relates specifically to devotional practices, symbols and magical techniques recorded as being associated with the goddess Hekate. These include amulets and charms, *defixiones* (binding curses), dreams, *goēteia* (sorcery), *nekuia* (divination from the dead), oracles, *pharmakeia* (herbal/poison magic), *rhizotomoi* (root-magic) and *theurgia* (divine working).

Hekate's liminality can clearly be seen throughout her entire history. Her three faces and three forms represent the three realms over which she had power. Her magic reached from the heavens above to the infernal realms below. She was the goddess of the crossroads, of thresholds, of dreams and oracles, of the realms of life and death. Initiatrix and Mistress of Magic, her myths and powers reach out to us today from long forgotten places, and will continue to be with humanity for many generations to come.

We hope that this book opens up doorways and pathways for you on your own journey through life.

Sorita d'Este & David Rankine

May 2009, Powys, Wales

THE GODDESS HEKATE, LAGINA
WITH KIND PERMISSION OF ALAN O'FLYNN

CHAPTER 1

FROM THE THREE-WAYS

The goddess Hekate was one of the most significant deities of the ancient world. Her history stretches back across the millennia. We find traces of her in the recent past, through into the Renaissance – stretching back through the Byzantine and Roman Empires, Hellenistic, Classical and Archiac Greece through into the Greek Dark Ages – and beyond. Hekate has been with us for at least three thousand years.

She was a liminal goddess who was present at all the boundaries and transitional moments in life. She was also an apotropaic (*'evil-averting'*) protector and guide, as illustrated by some of the many titles she was given. Hekate's triple form emphasised her power over the three realms, these being the heavens, sea and earth. Her primal nature was seen in the many animal heads she was depicted with, each emphasising different qualities of her manifold character.

Hekate was associated with ceremonies of initiation into the mysteries across the ancient world. This included the famous mysteries of Eleusis, and Selinus on the island of Sicily, as well as those on the Greek islands of Samothrace, Argos and Aigina.

Hekate has been given numerous epithets describing her roles and qualities over the thousands of years of her worship. Some of her well known titles include:

- Chthonia (*'earthly one'*),
- Dadouchos (*'torch-bearer'*),
- Enodia (*'of the ways'*),
- Kleidouchos (*'key-bearer'*),
- Kourotrophos (*'child's nurse'*)
- Phosphorus (*'light-bearer'*).
- Propolos (*'companion'*)
- Propylaia (*'before the gate'*),
- Soteira (*'saviour'*)
- Triformis (*'three bodied'*)
- Trioditis (*'of the three ways'*),

There was a major Hekate temple in the city of Lagina in Caria, which is in modern day Turkey. Each year in Lagina a ceremony was held called the *kleidos agoge* (*'procession of the key'*). Sarah Iles Johnston, author of *Hekate Soteira*, suggested this was connected to Hekate in her role as *Propylaia*, guarding the gates.[1] Additionally the name of this ceremony also recalls her title of *Kleidouchos*, for she bore the keys to the underworld, and determined who went to the paradisiacal part known as the Elysian Fields. In this context she oversaw the end of the journey for the soul of the deceased. The Orphic Hymn to Hekate went as far as to call her *"Keyholding Mistress of the whole world."*[2]

Her importance in the city of Lagina suggested she may well have fulfilled the role of tutelary goddess of the city, in the same way that the goddess Cybele did for Phrygia, and the Sumerian deities like Inanna did for the first city-states of the earliest Sumerian civilization.

---

1 See Restless Dead, Johnston, 1999, p206.
2 Orphic Hymn to Hekate, C1st-3rd CE, trans. Z. Yardley.

By the fifth century BCE Hekate had a temple at the gates of the city of Miletus, fifty miles to the northwest of Lagina, where her worship was already established there around a hundred years earlier. At Aphrodisias, which was also near Lagina, her worship had similarly been established by the fifth century BCE. Her role as guardian of the gate became so popular that the Romano-Greek historian Plutarch recorded a tale in the first century CE of one General berating another for putting a military trophy on a city gate, telling him he would have done better to erect a statue of Hekate instead.

As *Propylaia* (the one before the gate) she was an apotropaic guardian, averting evil and protecting those within. In this role shrines to her were found not only at the entrances to cities, temples and sanctuaries to other deities, but also to people's homes. The small shrine found outside the front door protecting the home was called a *hekataion*.

It has been pointed out that the geographic region of Caria in Asia Minor (where we can first trace her worship) had an extraordinarily large number of theophoric (lit. *'god-bearing'*) personal names with the Hekat- root. This further supports the idea that this area was an important one in her worship, as you would expect such a concentration of names somewhere closely linked her. The total number of names with the Hekat- root for Asia Minor was 310, with the number dropping to 158 for the Aegean Islands, and then down to Attica with 11.[3] It is also worth noting that the city of Idrias near Lagina was

---

3 Figures from Greek Personal Names: Their Value as Evidence, Hornblower & Matthews, 2000.

originally called Hekatesia. In a modern example of the continuation of Hekate's mysteries, this name (Hekatesia) has been adopted for an annual festival at the full moon in September now held at the Lagina temple since 2000, following its excavation in the 1990s.

In the region of Thrace, to the north of Caria, Hekate was both a powerful and popular goddess by the fifth century BCE. One of the earliest references to Hekate in Thrace is found in a hymn fragment about the city of Abdera, written by the ancient Greek lyrical poet Pindar. This dates to around the middle of the fifth century BCE and said:

> "It was the first of the month[4] when this befell, and the gracious Hekate, the maid of the ruddy feet, was thereby sending us a message that was longing for fulfilment."[5]

As we know from numerous literary references that Hekate was being worshipped in Athens in the fifth century BCE, it seems likely that her worship spread around the Aegean Sea very quickly during the end of the sixth century BCE and through into the fifth century BCE. From the literary references in the Greek oral poet Hesiod's *Theogony* in the eighth/seventh century BCE and the *Homeric Hymn to Demeter* in the seventh century BCE, we see an explosion of literary references in the fifth century BCE, showing that Hekate had truly become a significant part of Greek culture.

---

4 The first of the month, being the New Moon, a date which was often associated with Hekate
5 Paean 2, Pindar, 462 BCE, trans. G. Sandys.

So how can we trace Hekate back beyond her first appearance in Greece in the eight century BCE in Hesiod's *Theogony*? It has been suggested, by Von Rudloff in his book *Hekate in Ancient Greek Religion*, that a triad of names on one of the Linear B tablets from the Bronze Age may be linked to Hekate with the other Eleusinian goddesses of Persephone and Demeter. Linear B tablet *Tn316* from the Greek southern coastal city of Pylos, which has been dated to the thirteenth century BCE, contains the names Iphimedeia, Pereswa and Diwija amongst its list of deities. Of these, the first is probably an alternative name for Hekate, recalling her connection to Iphigenia (who was called Iphimede in the eighth century BCE *Catalogue of Women*), the second has been suggested as coming from the same root as Persephone, and the third may mean *'bright goddess'* or *'wealthy goddess'*, a title of Demeter.

Another clue to Hekate's origins may be found in her connection to lions. Although the images of Hekate flanked by lions are not amongst the earliest of her, they do hint at Middle Eastern origins, where they were a common feature. Goddesses were often depicted flanked by lions in imagery from the Middle East, as can be seen from examining the iconography of goddesses such as Inanna, Astarte and Cybele. However we must bear in mind that Artemis was also depicted flanked by big cats, and based on their age the Hekate images may be the result of her syncretisation with Artemis. Of course Artemis may also have roots in the Middle East, so this does not invalidate the possibility of Hekate's roots being further afield.

The lion references with Hekate include a frieze at the Lagina temple, coins showing her with lions, and also later references from the *Chaldean Oracles* and the *Greek Magical Papyri*, showing the persistence of the association. In the *Chaldean Oracles* Hekate is described as being *"lion-possessing"*,[6] and even more significantly we see, *"If you call upon Me often you will perceive everything in lion-form."*[7]

In the '*Prayer to Selene for any Spell*' in the *Greek Magical Papyri*, which by its content can be seen to be more of a Hekate spell, we find the phrase *"you stand protected by two rampant lions"*.[8]

The fact that dogs were sacrificed to Hekate has also been presented as evidence for her non-Greek origins, as the practice of dog sacrifice was only found in relation to foreign gods who became part of the Greek pantheon, another such example being sacrifices made to the god Ares. Fritz Graf wrote about this phenomenon in his essay '*What is new about Greek sacrifice?*' saying that dog sacrifice carried its own message of liminality:

> *"Well over ninety percent of all sacrificed animals came from four species: bovines, goats, sheep, and swine. Any animal which did not belong into this norm-group became semantically important – as, e.g., the dog."*[9]

As well as the worship of Hekate in conjunction with Demeter and Persephone at Eleusis, there was also a temple of these three goddesses at Selinus in Sicily. It seems likely that the worship there may have

---

6 Chaldean Oracles, C2nd CE, trans. S. Ronan.
7 Chaldean Oracles, C2nd CE, trans. S. Ronan.
8 PGM IV.2811-12, trans. Krause.
9 What is new about Greek sacrifice?, Graf, 2002

taken a similar form to that at Eleusis. We know that Hekate was also worshipped on the islands of Aigina, Argos and Samothrace, though we do not know the form the worship took at these places.

When examining the origins of Hekate from an archaeological and literary perspective, we have to also consider the origins ascribed to her, at different times, within the various recorded mythological stories. In Hesiod's *Theogony* it was the goddess of the stars Asteria and her husband Perses who were credited as being the parents of Hekate:

> *"Asteria [Starry One] of happy name, whom Perses [Destroyer] once led to his great house to be called his dear wife. And she conceived and bare Hekate."*[10]

Asteria was associated with the night sky, both through astrology and also her role as giver of prophetic dreams. The temple of Asteria on Delos was known for dream incubation. This connection to oracles and dreams was one which would be passed on to her daughter Hekate. Asteria was also sister to Leto, the mother by Zeus of the divine twins Artemis and Apollo, who were Hekate's cousins. Hekate's relationship to Artemis in particular would become very close to the point of the goddesses being equated.

Although Perses was usually translated as 'Destroyer', we may also observe that Perses was used to mean 'Persian'. In his fifth century BCE work *Histories*, the Greek geographer Herodotus described the Persians being named after Perses, son of Perseus. So from this perspective we can speculate that Hekate's father was viewed as being Persian, i.e. from the Middle East. A number of sources gave variants of

---

10 Theogony, Hesiod, C8th BCE, trans. H.G. Evelyn-White.

the name Perses for her father, such as Persaios and Perseus, as will be seen from the subsequent quotes.

The seventh century BCE *Homeric Hymn to Demeter*, maintained the view given in the *Theogony*, calling her *"Tender-hearted Hekate, bright-coiffed, the daughter of Persaios."*[11]

The majority of authors perpetuated this most popular attribution in their own writings, through to Pseudo-Apollodorus in his *Bibliotheca* in the second century CE. He wrote that Hekate was *"The maiden daughter of Perseus, Brimo Trimorphos."*[12] The titles *Brimo* ('*angry*' or '*terrifying*') and *Trimorphos* ('*three-formed*' or '*three-bodied*') were two of the many applied to her. Hekate was often associated with triplicity, and this would be a recurrent theme in her worship and magic:

> *"And you who oft frequent the triple way and rule the triple decades with three forms and flames and dogs."*[13]

A Scholiast[14] on Apollonius Rhodius' classic *Argonautica* gave a range of possible parents. It reported that the *Orphic Hymns* attributed Deo (Demeter) as her mother, Bacchylides attributed Nyx as her mother, Mousaios attributed Zeus and Asteria as her parents and Pherecydes gave Aristaios as her father.

These alternative attributions of parentage are all more connected than they might initially seem. That the *Orphic Hymns* should attribute Demeter as mother

---

11 Homeric Hymn to Demeter, C7th BCE, trans. H.G. Evelyn-White.
12 Alexandria, Lycophron, C3rd BCE, trans. Mair.
13 PGM IV.2528-30.
14 A Scholiast is an explanatory note or comment, usually on an ancient Greek or Latin text.

to Hekate is unsurprising, when we take into account the assimilation of the *Homeric Hymn to Demeter* into the Orphic Mysteries. From that viewpoint it was entirely logical to bring Hekate more closely into the family of goddesses who were central to the powers of the underworld, and hence key to the process of transmigration of souls, to reincarnate again. This was a significant part of the Orphic Mysteries.

Nyx (*'Night'*) was equated to Asteria, for what is night if not the starry sky? Nyx was one of the first primeval gods, from whom the race of gods were born. Zeus likewise was an obvious suggestion for parent as the father of many of the main Greek gods, and also the central figure in the *Chaldean Oracles* with Hekate.

Aristaios was an interesting choice, being a god associated with medical herbs, who gave the world honey, mead, olives and cheese-making. He was usually described as being the son of Apollo by Cyrene, though Bacchylides attributed his parentage to the earth goddess Ge and the celestial Ouranos.

The deities honoured in the religions of ancient Greece and Rome were not usually worshipped in isolation. Thus Hekate was frequently found in the company of other deities, such as Hermes, Apollo, Demeter, Persephone, Cybele, Mithras and others. An inscription from Rome in the fourth century CE makes this point clearly:

> *"The most potent lord Sextilius Agesilaus Aedesius ... father of the unconquered sun god Mithras, hierophant of Hecate, chief shepherd of Dionysus, reborn forever through sacrifice of bulls and rams*

consecrated the altar to the great gods, to the mother of the gods and to Attis."[15]

Another inscription from Rome in the same period makes it clear that there was a mystery cult associated with Hekate, as there was with the Indo-Iranian god Mithras and the Phrygian goddess Cybele, and at Eleusis. In this instance, the priestess Paulina was an initiate of several mystery cults:

> *"Initiate of Ceres and the Eleusinian [Mysteries], initiate of Hecate at Aegina, tauroboliata, hierophant."*[16]

The gods particularly associated with Hekate were the other chthonic ones, i.e. Hermes, Hades, Persephone, and Ge, as well as Zeus, Rhea, Demeter, Mithras and Cybele, and the solar gods Helios and Apollo. The chthonic gods Hermes, Hades, Persephone and Ge were also those who were found most often on the *defixiones* (curse tablets). Zeus and Rhea both feature in the *Chaldean Oracles*, especially Zeus as the supreme deity.

Over time some goddesses were partially or fully assimilated into Hekate. These were Brimo, Despoina, Enodia, Genetyllis, Kotys, Kratais and Kourotrophos. She was also syncretised with or equated to Artemis, Selene, Mene, Persephone, Physis, Bendis, Bona Dea, Diana, Ereschigal and Isis.

Hekate and Hermes were often associated, as Hermes was the most liminal of the male gods in the Greek pantheon. Hermes Chthonia was often invoked together with Hekate Chthonia on the *defixiones*. The

---

15 CIL VI.510, 367 CE.
16 Inscription from the tomb of Fabia Aconia Paulina, C4th CE, trans. M.R. Lefkowitz.

Greek geographer Pausanias recorded seeing statues of the couple as Hermes Propylaios and Hekate Propylaia at the gates to the city of Athens.[17]

In the *Greek Magical Papyri* there was even an instance of their names being combined, in a restraining spell,[18] which declared *"Entrapper, Mistress of Corpses, Hermes, Hekate, Hermekate,"*.

Helios was also associated with Hekate in various tales. With Hekate, Helios was the only other god to be aware of Persephone's abduction in the *Homeric Hymn to Demeter*. The two were also inked in a hymn fragment from the lost fifth century BCE play *The Root-Cutters*, by the Greek tragedian Sophocles:

> *O Lord Helios and Sacred Fire*
> *The spear of Hekate of the Crossroads*
> *Which she bears as she travels Olympus*
> *And dwells in the triple ways of the holy land*
> *She who is crowned with oak-leaves*
> *And the coils of wild serpents.* [19]

Helios was the most commonly invoked god in the *Greek Magical Papyri* (sometimes syncretised with Apollo), as Hekate was the most commonly invoked goddess. Helios and Hekate are also both given in different sources as the parents to the sorceresses Circe and Medea, though not at the same time. In one account Helios was the grandfather of Hekate, who was the mother of the two sorceresses:

> *"We are told that Helios had two sons, Aeetes and Perses, Aeetes being the king of Kolkhis and the other king of the Tauric Khersonese, ... Perses had a*

---

17 Description of Greece, Pausanias, C2nd CE, trans. Frazer.
18 PGM III.1-164.
19 The Root-Cutters, Sophocles, C5th BCE, trans. Z. Yardley.

daughter Hekate ... she married Aeetes and bore two daughters, Circe and Medea, and a son Aigialeus."[20]

When Medea swears her oath in the *Argonautica* she also links Helios and Hekate:

"I swear by Helios' sacred light and by the secret rites of Perses' night-wandering daughter [Hekate]."[21]

Zeus had a long-standing association with Hekate. From the *Theogony*, where he *"gave her splendid gifts, to have a share of the earth, and the unfruitful sea. She received honour also in starry jeaven, and is honoured exceedingly by the deathless gods."*[22] He was also at times said to be her father, and together they form the central deities of the Chaldean Oracles, with Hekate being the intermediary power as Soteira (*'saviour'*) transmitting the divine influence of the supreme Zeus to all the worlds and beings.

Hekate was sometimes identified with the sea goddess Kratais, who was the mother of the monster Scylla, making Hekate her mother as well. This connection was emphasised by Kratais also being called *Skylakagetis* (*'Leader of the Dogs'*). In Apollonius Rhodius' *Argonautica* we see Circe telling her niece Medea:

"Nor let them go too near the hateful den of Ausonian Skylla, that wicked monster borne to Phorkys by night-wandering Hekate, whom men call Kratais."[23]

This does of course contrast with the common view that Hekate was an untouched maiden goddess, as

---

20 Library of History, Diodorus Siculus, C1st BCE, trans. Oldfather.
21 Argonautica 4.1018, Apollonius Rhodius, C3rd CE, trans. R.C. Seaton.

22 Theogony, Hesiod, C8th BCE, trans. H.G. Evelyn-White.

23 Argonautica, Book 4, Apollonius Rhodius, C3rd BCE, trans. Seaton.

expressed by Pseudo-Apollodorus in his *Bibliotheca* when he wrote that Hekate was *"The maiden daughter of Perseus."*[24] That there should be such a range of possibilities simply emphasises the unpredictable and liminal nature of Hekate.

Literary Sources

The literary sources referring to Hekate span a period of more than two thousand years. We have included a list of all the texts referred to in this book in chronological order for the convenience of the reader.

Date	Source
C9th BCE	*Odyssey*, Homer
C8th BCE	*Theogony*, Hesiod
C8th BCE	*Works and Days*, Hesiod
C7th BCE	*Homeric Hymn to Demeter*
C7th BCE	*Fragments*, Alkman
C6th BCE	*Fragments*, Hipponax
Early C5th BCE	*Suppliants*, Aeschylus
C5th BCE	*The Nurses of Dionysus*, Aeschylus
C5th BCE	*Fragments*, Aeschylus
C5th BCE	*Life of Homer*, Herodotus
C5th BCE	*The Histories*, Herodotus
C5th BCE	*On the Sacred Disease*, Hippocrates
C5th BCE	*The Root-Cutters*, Sophocles

---

24 Alexandria, Lycophron, C3rd BCE, trans. Mair.

C5th BCE	*The Women who say they will expel the Goddess [Hekate]*, Sophron
C5th BCE	*Fragments*, Eupolis
C5th BCE	*Fragments*, Bacchylides
C5th BCE	*Purifications*, Empedocles
C5th BCE – C2nd CE	*Bacchic Gold Funeral Tablets*
462 BCE	*Pythian Odes 4*, Pindar
450 BCE	*The Choephori*, Aeschylus
442 BCE	*The Thracian Women*, Cratinus
431 BCE	*Medea*, Euripides
420 BCE	*The Wasps*, Aristophanes
414 BCE	*Iphigenia among the Taurians*, Euripides
412 BCE	*Helen*, Euripides
410 BCE	*Lysistrata*, Aristophanes
400 BCE	*Frogs*, Aristophanes
380 BCE	*Plutus*, Aristophanes
C4th BCE	*Memorabilia*, Xenophon
C4th BCE	*The Harp Maker*, Anaxilas
C4th BCE	*Characters*, Theophrastus
C4th BCE	*Enquiry into Plants*, Theophrastus
C4th BCE	*On Piety*, Theophrastus
C3rd BCE	*Argonautica*, Apollonius Rhodius

C3rd BCE	*Alexandria,* Lycophron
C3rd BCE	*Hymn 3 to Artemis,* Callimachus
270 BCE	*Idylls,* Theocritus
C2nd BCE	*Chronicle,* Apollodorus
C2nd BCE – C5th CE	*Greek Magical Papyri*
C1st BCE	*Library of History,* Diodorus Siculus
C1st BCE	*Carmina,* Catullus
c. 40 BCE	*Eclogues,* Virgil
35 BCE	*Satires,* Horace
30 BCE	*Epodes,* Horace
Late C1st BCE	*The Aeneid,* Virgil
8 CE	*Metamorphoses,* Ovid
8 CE	*Fasti,* Ovid
60 CE	*Pharsalia,* Lucan
C1st CE	*Medea,* Seneca
C1st CE	*Thebaid,* Statius
C1st CE	*Natural History,* Pliny
C1st CE	*Jewish Antiquities,* Flavius Josephus
C1st CE	*The Jewish War,* Flavius Josephus
C1st-3rd CE	*Orphic Hymn to Hekate*
Early C2nd CE	*Moralia,* Plutarch
Early C2nd CE	*Roman Questions,* Plutarch

C2nd CE	*On the Characteristics of Animals,* Aelian
C2nd CE	*Description of Greece,* Pausanias
C2nd CE	*Bibliotheca,* Pseudo-Apollodorus
C2nd CE	*Protrepticus,* Clement of Alexandria
C2nd CE	*Philopseudes,* Lucian
C2nd CE	*Metamorphoses,* Antoninus Liberalis
C2nd CE	*Address to the Greeks,* Tatian
C2nd CE	*The True Word,* Celsus
C2nd CE	*Chaldean Oracles*
C2nd CE	*Papyrus Oxyrynchus*
Late C2nd CE	*Metamorphoses (The Golden Ass),* Apuleius
Early C3rd CE	*The Life of Apollonius of Tyana,* Philostratus the Athenian
Early C3rd CE	*Stromata,* Clement of Alexandria
C3rd CE	*Philosophumena or The Refutation of All Heresies,* Hippolytus
C3rd CE	*On the Mysteries of the Egyptians,* Iamblichus
C3rd CE	*On Images,* Porphyry
C3rd CE	*On Abstinence,* Porphyry
C3rd CE	*Prophecy from Oracles,* Porphyry
C3rd CE	*Scholiast on the Cratylus of Plato,* Porphyry

C3rd CE	*The Deipnosophists*, Athanaeus
Early C4th CE	*Praeparatio Evangelica*, Eusebius
C4th CE	*Against the Heathen*, Arnobius
C4th CE	*Institutiones Divinae*, Lactantius
C4th CE	*Orphic Argonautica*
411 CE	*Sermon 241*, Augustine
Early C5th CE	*Hymns*, Synesius
C5th CE	*Dionysiaca*, Nonnus
C5th CE	*Saturnalia*, Macrobius
C5th CE	*Hymn to Hekate and Janus*, Proclus
C5th CE	*Life of Proclus*, Marinus
C5th CE	*Pistis Sophia*
Early C6th CE	*Celestial Hierarchy*, Pseudo-Dionysus the Areopagite
C6th CE	*Difficulties and Solutions of First Principles*, Damascius
C6th CE	*Liber De Mensibus*, John Lydus
C6th CE	*Ethnica*, Stephen of Byzantium
C10th CE	*Suda*, Unknown
C11th CE	*Commentary on the Chaldean Oracles*, Michael Psellus
C12th CE	*Scholiast on Alexandria of Lycophron*, John Tzetzes
1533	*Of Occult Philosophy*, Cornelius Agrippa

1571	*Le Imagini Degli Dei Degli Antichi,* Vicenzo Cartari
c.1606	*Macbeth,* William Shakespeare
1795	*A New and Complete Illustration of the Occult Sciences,* Ebenezer Sibly

CHAPTER 2

IN HER SERVICE

Hekate appeared frequently in the literature of the ancient world, in theological, legendary and fictional writings. Her roles and genealogy were described by philosophers whose views shaped the development of magic like Hesiod and Porphyry, and her abilities and epithets occurred in the tales of legendary heroines whose deeds are still enacted in plays and tales today, like the sorceresses Medea and Circe. From the literature of the time it seems that Hekate was frequently associated with the witches of Thessaly, whose fame spread to such an extent, that they are still known today. In the case of a root-magician like Empedocles, the link to Hekate is more speculative, though we may note that she was particularly associated with *rhizotomoi* (root-magic) and *pharmakeia* (herbal/poison magic), and he was a root-magician. This is illustrated by examples such as the Hekate invocation in the remaining fragment of the lost fifth century BCE Sophocles play, *The Root-Cutters*.

Hesiod

Hesiod's influence was highly significant to the development of ancient Greek religious and spiritual views through the material in his works. Of these, both from the eighth century BCE, two are particularly significant, *Works and Days* and the *Theogony*. The former work was influential on both the Orphic and Pythagorean schools of thought, being cited as part of their argument for a vegetarian diet. The *Theogony* was hugely important in setting out the first synthesised pattern of creation for the Greek gods, and giving the extremely significant first known literary description of Hekate. The central position of Zeus in the *Theogony* and importance of Hekate would be mirrored a thousand years later in the *Chaldean Oracles*, with both texts also being presented as divine revelation.

It has been suggested that Hesiod was a devotee of Hekate, hence the inclusion of the uniquely large and tremendously positive section about her in the *Theogony*. Alternatively it has been suggested that the Hekate section was inserted into the *Theogony* by somebody else, at a later date, for the same reason.

We know that Hesiod's brother's name was Perses, which is of course the name given for Hekate's father. Considering the acrimony with which Hesiod wrote about his brother in *Works and Days*, it could be speculated that his brother was named after Hekate's father, and that Hesiod's family worshipped Hekate as their tutelary goddess.

Empedocles

The fifth century BCE Greek root-magician and philosopher Empedocles (c.495-c.435 BCE), invented the doctrine of the four elements of air, fire, water and earth which has been perpetuated through to modern magic. There are circumstantial hints in his practices suggesting that he may have been a devotee of Hekate, as can be seen by examining his life. Empedocles claimed a range of abilities, which are particularly interesting when we consider the powers attributed in the legends to Hekate and her devotees. He declared that he could teach remedies against old age, a deed performed by Medea for Jason's father Aeson. He also claimed the power to control the weather, and the witches of Thessaly were famed for their ability to draw down the moon from heaven. Finally Empedocles stated that he could bring back the dead, a power attributed to Hekate as bearer of the keys to the underworld.

Empedocles claimed to be immortal, and was said to have jumped into the volcano Mount Etna on his homeland of Sicily, with only a bronze sandal left floating in the lava to show his passing. The bronze sandal was a cult symbol of Hekate.

The name *Purifications* (*Katharmoi*) given to one of the two fragments of Empedocles' work remaining, is interesting as purification was particularly associated with Hekate. Diodorus of Ephesus recounted a story about Empedocles, saying that he stopped a plague caused by bad river water at Selinus (where the temple to Hekate, Demeter and Persephone was based), by paying for two other rivers to be diverted so their water purified the first river. This major labour, funded out of his own pocket, successfully ended the plague. This could also indicate that he was an initiate of the mysteries celebrated at the temple of Hekate, Demeter and Persephone situated there.

Porphyry

The third century CE philosopher Porphyry of Tyre (234-c.305 CE) was a Phoenician Neo-Platonist who studied under Plotinus. He wrote widely on a range of subjects including philosophy, vegetarianism, oracles, anti-Christian rhetoric and logic. His *Introduction* was used for many centuries as a standard work on logic in both Europe and the Arab world.

Porphyry was influenced by the *Chaldean Oracles*, which helped define his view of Hekate, and this may provide a possible insight into why she occurred so often in his writings. In his *Scholiast on the Cratylus of Plato*, he described Hekate in a manner which not only exhorted her superiority, but also demonstrated knowledge of the *Chaldean Oracles* and the divine hierarchy contained within them, such as the connection between Hekate and souls and virtues as their source:

> *"Likewise, according to an essence transcending the other powers of this triple vivific order, the dominion of Hecate is established; but according to a middle power, and which is generative of wholes, that of soul; and, according to intellectual conversion, that of Virtue."*[25]

Porphyry was a staunch vegetarian, writing two works on the subject, *On Abstinence*, and *On the Impropriety of Killing Living Beings for Food*. He frequently referred to Hekate in his writings, thus his *Prophecy from Oracles* contained an oracle from Hekate on Jesus. The Christian theologian Eusebius quoted fragments of Porphyry extensively in his *Praeparatio Evangelica*, and this included instructions on her symbols and how to make a shrine to Hekate and her worship.

---

25 Scholiast on the Cratylus of Plato, Porphyry, C3rd CE, trans. Taylor.

Hekate was mentioned significantly in *On Abstinence*, in the tale of the holiest man who did not sacrifice animals, but offered fragrances and cakes to Hekate and Hermes. Porphyry when commenting on the various gods, emphasised the benefits of Hekate when he also observed:

> *"But Hecate, when invoked by the names of a bull, a dog, and a lioness, is more propitious."*[26]

Porphyry's views were influenced by his teacher Plotinus, and a result of this was the dialogue between Porphyry and his disciple Iamblichus, which would produce the latter's classic work on theurgy, *On the Mysteries of the Egyptians*.

Circe

> *"Perses had a daughter Hekate ... she married Aeetes and bore two daughters, Circe and Medea, and a son Aigialeus."*[27]

Circe stands out as the first great fictional sorceress or witch of Greek literature, with a range of magical abilities corresponding to her semi-divine status and relationship with Hekate. These included controlling the weather, love magic, necromancy, the ability to move unseen, shapeshifting, control of animals and herbal lore.

Indeed Odysseus was only able to defeat Circe's shapeshifting magic by the use of an herb given to him by the god Hermes, and even then he was still susceptible to her charms, staying with her for a year. According to a scholiast to Lycophron's *Alexandria*,

---

26 On Abstinence, Porphyry, C3rd CE, trans. Taylor.
27 Library of History, Diodorus Siculus, C1st BCE, trans. Oldfather.

Circe raised the ghost of Odysseus after he was dead, reminding us that even death did not protect a person from the attention of powerful magicians.

Circe was always portrayed as a priestess of Hekate, and according to some sources she was said to be her daughter. In the *Argonautica*, Circe performed purificatory rites on her niece Medea and Jason, ordered by Zeus, in atonement for Jason killing Medea's brother Apsyrtus. Circe's magical abilities as a priestess were emphasised by this deed, which was presaged by bloody visions symbolising the murder and the need for purification:

> "First, to atone for the murder still unexpiated, she held above their heads the young of a sow whose dugs yet swelled from the fruit of the womb, and, severing its neck, sprinkled their hands with the blood; and again she made propitiation with other drink offerings, calling on Zeus the Cleanser, the protector of murder-stained suppliants. And all the defilements in a mass her attendants bore forth from the palace - the Naiad nymphs who ministered all things to her. And within, Circe, standing by the hearth, kept burning atonement-cakes without wine, praying the while that she might stay from their wrath the terrible Furies, and that Zeus himself might be propitious and gentle to them both."[28]

Medea

Medea was possibly the greatest tragic heroine, or villainess, depending on the teller, of the literature of the ancient world. In some versions of the stories, Medea was described as the daughter of Hekate, and she named the goddess as *"the mistress whom I*

---

28 Argonautica, Book 4, Apollonius Rhodius, C3rd BCE, trans. Seaton.

worship above all others and name as my helper."[29] In all the tales where she appeared, Medea was a priestess of Hekate:

> *"As a rule she [Medea] did not spend her time at home, but was busy all day in the temple of Hekate, of whom she was priestess."*[30]

Medea set a new pattern in literature, as a beautiful and powerful female witch who could not only bring the dead back to life, but rejuvenate the elderly. She rejuvenated Jason and his father Aeson, the nurses of Dionysus[31] and a ram, and then deliberately gave the wrong spell to Pelias' daughters causing them to kill their father. This ability was associated with Medea from the earliest tales, being seen in a fragment of the lost epic *Nostoi* (*Homecomings*), where she cooked up herbs in a golden cauldron. She emphasised the assistance of Hekate in her magic, saying, *"provided the triple-formed goddess helps and by her presence assents to my great experiments."*[32]

Two other aspects of Medea's tale should also be mentioned. These are the fact that when Medea fled she was accepted as ruler by the people who then took her name, the Medes. Also significant is her oracular role, predicting the colonisation of Thera, a prediction which was subsequently repeated by the Delphic Oracle. When this prediction was made, Pindar upgraded Medea, for he had her speaking words from her *"immortal mouth"*.[33]

---

29 Medea, Euripides, 431 BCE, trans. F. Graf.
30 Argonautica, Book 4, Apollonius Rhodius, C3rd BCE, trans. Seaton.
31 The Nurses of Dionysus, Aeschylus, C5th BCE, trans. J.G. Frazer.
32 Metamorphoses, Ovid, 8 CE, trans. C.E. Newlands.
33 Pythian Ode 4, Pindar, 462 BCE, trans. N Krevans.

Medea was a significant figure, not only in the number of times she appeared in tales, but also for the accompanying descriptions of her actions, which provide a rich source of contextual information regarding magical practices. Fortunately for us, when the poets wrote their tales, they set their material within the context of their society to ensure ease of understanding in their audiences. Thus over a period of centuries Medea was portrayed in stories such as Apollonius Rhodius' *Argonautica*, Euripides' *Medea*, Seneca's *Medea*, and Ovid's *Metamorphoses*.

The Witches of Thessaly

Although the witches of Thessaly were not a priesthood of Hekate, they were often linked with her as expert practitioners of the types of magic particularly associated with the goddess, such as *nekuia* ('*divination from the dead*'), *goēteia* ('*sorcery*') and *pharmakeia* ('*herbal/poison magic*'). In Lucan's *Pharsalia*, from the first century CE, his witch Erictho made a proprietary claim on Hekate as being associated with the witches of Thessaly when she declared:

> "*Persephone, who dost detest heaven and thy mother, and who art the lowest form of our Hecate.*"[34]

This quote is interesting, not only in the equation of Persephone to Hekate, but also the implication that Persephone enjoyed the underworld and the company of her husband Hades, detesting heaven and Demeter (her mother). The association of Thessaly (in northern Greece) with magic was even seen in the *Greek Magical*

---

34 Pharsalia, Lucan, 60 CE, trans. J.D. Duff

Papyri, with several necromantic charms attributed to Pitys, a Thessalian king.[35]   Lucan emphasised the magical nature of Thessaly in *Pharsalia* when he wrote:

> *"The earth of Thessaly produces poisonous herbs in the mountains, and the rocks feel it when magicians sing their deadly spells. Many plants grow there that may compel the gods, and the woman who came from Colchis [Medea] picked in Thessalian country many herbs that she did not bring along."[36]*

Of the famous witches in literature associated with Hekate, Erictho was a Thessalian witch, and Medea gathered her herbs there.   By the time of Horace the term *Thessalian* had become synonymous with '*magical*', hence in the child sacrifice scene in *Epodes* with Canidia and her fellow witches, the Italian witch Folia speaks the charms, and, *"brings down the enchanted stars and the moon from the sky with Thessalian voice."[37]*

Lampads

The seventh century BCE Spartan lyric poet Alkman mentioned a group of torch-bearing nymphs who were companions to Hekate.[38]   These nymphs, who were called Lampads, were not mentioned anywhere else, but the early date must make us wonder if this was the last mention of an existing tradition. Thus they might, for example, represent the torch-bearing priestesses of Hekate, like those at Eleusis.

---

35 PGM IV.1928-2005, PGM IV.2006-2125, & PGM IV.2140-44.
36 Pharsalia, Lucan, 60 CE, trans. G. Luck.
37 Epodes, Horace, 30 BCE, trans. M Meyer.
38 Fragment 63, Alkman, C7th BCE.

Hekate's Vegetarian Followers

Significantly, all of the philosophers previously mentioned who referred to Hekate in their writings were staunch vegetarians. Empedocles, who believed in the transmigration of souls, argued that to eat a living creature was a grievous sin, as you were eating another soul on the journey to divinity. He maintained the Golden Age of the past had been one without animal sacrifice or the consumption of meat. Rather the offerings to the gods were substances such as the sweet resins of frankincense and myrrh, and honey.

Empedocles was so passionate about the subject, that in his work *Purifications*, of which only fragments survive, he wrote of meat consumption:

> *"Will you not cease from the din of slaughter? Do you not see that you are devouring each other in the heedlessness of your minds? ... Alas that the pitiless day did not destroy me first, before I contrived the wretched deed of eating flesh with my lips."*[39]

The belief that the Golden Age was fleshless was first postulated by Hesiod in his eighth century BCE *Works and Days*. Hesiod emphasised the vegetarian diet of the Golden Age, saying:

> *"The fruitful grainland yielded its harvest to them of its own accord; this was great and abundant."*[40]

Other fourth century BCE Pythagorean philosophers such as the cartographer Dicaearchus of Messana, and his friend the naturalist Theophrastus were also vegetarians who wrote on vegetarianism and the Golden Age. Theophrastus, in his work *On Piety*, perpetuated the views of Hesiod.

---

39 Purifications, Empedocles, C5th BCE, trans. G.S. Kirk.
40 Works and Days, Hesiod, C8th BCE, trans. R. Lattimore.

Porphyry was vehement in his vegetarianism, and wrote two works supporting this viewpoint, *On Abstinence*, and *On the Impropriety of Killing Living Beings for Food*. It is also interesting to observe that Porphyry's teachers, the noted philosophers Plotinus and Plutarch were both vegetarian.

Porphyry recounted a tale in *On Abstinence* which emphasised a move away from animal sacrifice and towards using incense, vegetables and first fruits, perhaps in an effort to try and restore practices to the way they were perceived in the Golden Age:

> *"crowning and adorning the statues of Hermes and Hecate, and the other sacred images which were left to us by our ancestors, and that he also honoured the Gods with frankincense, and sacred wafers and cakes."*[41]

The Roman philosophers Seneca and Ovid, both of whom wrote significant works treating the tale of Medea (*Medea* and *Metamorphoses* respectively), with her devotion to Hekate, were vegetarian as well.

---

41 On Abstinence, Porphyry, C3rd CE, trans. T. Taylor.

CHAPTER 3

SACRED ELEUSIS

Eleusis was like the Vatican City of its day, a hugely influential and powerful religious centre. At Eleusis a mystery cult celebrated the Greater and Lesser Mysteries, which incorporated the tale of the grain goddess Demeter and her daughter Persephone. Becoming an initiate of the Eleusinian Mysteries was an important social and spiritual act, for not only did it give a certain status to be an initiate of the Mysteries, but it was also said to ensure a positive afterlife in the underworld, where Persephone was queen.

The worship of Hekate was intertwined with the mysteries of Eleusis, along with Demeter and Persephone. The Greek scholar Apollodorus recorded in his *Chronicle* that when King Ericthonius died, his son Pandion became king, and during his reign Demeter came to Attica and was welcomed by King Celeus at Eleusis.[42] This placed Demeter at Eleusis during the period 1462-1423 BCE.

Later in the *Chronicle* reference was made to the first celebration of the Mysteries at Eleusis in the reign of King Erechtheus, around 1409 BCE. So if the presence of Hekate in the Eleusinian Mysteries was not a late addition, we may assume that she was present from the beginning of the Mysteries. This would place

---

42 Chronicle III.XIV.7, Apollodorus, C2nd BCE.

her in Greece in the fifteenth century BCE, some seven hundred years before the first literary reference in the *Theogony*.

Hekate's involvement in the Eleusinian Mysteries cannot be ignored. Although there are a myriad of theories on the exact nature of the mysteries and rituals which took place at the Greater and Lesser Eleusinian Mysteries, it cannot be disputed that it was a very important spiritual centre. The priesthood there owned large areas of land, were tremendously wealthy and wielded political power throughout the known world. We know from archaeological findings that the sanctuary at Eleusis may have been in use as early as 1500 BCE, supporting the timescale of Apollodorus' *Chronicle*.

A smaller temple, which stood at the entrance to the main temple, was according to the Greek geographer Pausanias dedicated to Artemis *Propylaia* and the sea god Poseidon. *Propylaia* was one of Hekate's key titles, and this temple may have been dedicated to Hekate and Poseidon, rather than Artemis. Artemis was not referred to by this title anywhere else, and she did not have any obvious associations with the mysteries of Persephone and Demeter as enacted at Eleusis.

Additionally Hekate was linked to Poseidon in other writings, including the *Theogony*, and fish were often offered to her in sacrificial rites. Further evidence which indicated Hekate's role at this sanctuary comes from a vase found at the site which depicted a young female figure, holding two torches, a pose called *The Running Maiden* and which is now widely accepted as being a depiction of Hekate.

The *Homeric Hymn to Demeter* was effectively the canon of the Eleusinian mystery told through the tale of the Abduction of Persephone. So let us recount that tale to make the light of Hekate clearer.

Hades was lonely in his role as underworld god, and made an agreement with his brother, Zeus, the ruler of the gods. Hades would abduct his daughter Persephone and make her his bride. To do this he created the beautiful narcissus flower as a lure for her, and the earth goddess Ge grew it as a favour to him. When Persephone was out picking flowers with some of the other maiden goddesses including Athena and Artemis on the Plain of Nysa, she spotted the narcissus and wandered off to pick it. Seizing the moment, Hades came out of the earth in his chariot and abducted Persephone, taking her back into the underworld. The only witnesses were Hekate, who heard the struggle from her cave, and Helios the sun god, who saw it all from the sky.

Persephone called out to her mother from the underworld, and Demeter searched the earth unsuccessfully for nine days looking for her daughter. On the tenth day Hekate approached her and told her what she had heard of the struggle, and suggested they speak to Helios. Helios recounted the whole scene, including informing her that Zeus was responsible for the abduction, but tried to persuade Demeter it was a good match for her daughter. Demeter was inconsolable and wandered the earth, ending up at Eleusis, where she took the role of nursemaid to Queen Metaneira's son Demophon, disguised as an old woman.

Demeter would not eat or drink until princess Iambê made her laugh by telling her obscene jokes, and Metaneira offered her honeyed wine, but she refused it. Instead she told Metaneira to mix barley, water and pennyroyal and make the drink *kykeon*, which she drank. Demeter nourished the baby prince Demophon, feeding him on ambrosia and placing him in the flames of the fire every night to make him immortal. One night Queen Metaneira saw this and shrieked in horror, disturbing Demeter. Demeter revealed her divinity and chastised her, saying that Demophon would now be mortal like any other human. She instructed the queen to build a temple to her and that her rites (the Eleusinian mysteries) would be celebrated there. When the temple was built Demeter took up residence in it, and prevented anything from growing for the year, so there were no crops and humanity suffered terribly.

From Olympus, Zeus saw the suffering of humanity, and sent Iris, the messenger of the gods, to summon Demeter. Demeter ignored the summons and all the other gods who came to her offering her gifts to return to Olympus, saying she would not move until she had her daughter back, and neither would the crops grow again.

Zeus then sent Hermes to negotiate with Hades for the return of Persephone. However Hades persuaded Persephone to eat a few pomegranate seeds, binding her to the underworld. Persephone was reunited with her mother and they rejoiced. Hekate joined them and welcomed Persephone back, and from that time she became her guide (*Propolos*) on her annual journey to and from the underworld. For Zeus ordered that due to the pomegranate seeds she had eaten she now was constrained to spend one third of the year in the underworld with her husband Hades, and the other two thirds with her mother Demeter. That is why the earth was barren for one third of the year, as Demeter mourned the time her daughter was in the underworld away from her.

It is significant that during the abduction, only Hekate and Helios were aware that anything was happening. So not only did Hekate hear a distant struggle when none of the other gods did, indicating a keener perception of unseen events, but her connection to the seen and unseen paths of nature was implied by her being *"the one who keeps in mind the vigour of nature"*. Thus when describing the cries of Persephone during her abduction, the *Homeric Hymn* said:

> *"But not one of the immortal ones, or of human mortals, heard her voice. Not even the olive trees which bear their splendid harvest. Except for the daughter of Persaios, the one who keeps in mind the vigour of nature. She heard it from her cave. She is Hekate, with the splendid headband."*[43]

Another interesting point made by the scholar Athanassakis in his translation of the *Homeric Hymn* was that there could have been an early reference to the association between Hekate and the Moon. He claimed this was implied by the line:

> *"But when the tenth light-bringing Dawn came to her, Hekate carrying a light in her hands, met her,"*[44]

However this line could also refer to the suggested attribution of Venus as the morning star to Hekate as one of her torches, as this is the last star seen in the sky at dawn before the day sky is supreme.

---

43 Homeric Hymn to Demeter, C7th BCE, trans. Gregory Nagy.
44 Homeric Hymn to Demeter, C7th BCE, trans. Athanassakis.

The Orphic version of the hymn had some interesting and relevant variations to the Homeric Hymn. Instead of Persephone being abducted on the Plain of Nysa, she was abducted at Eleusis. Nysa was the name of more than one place, and significantly there was a Plain of Nysa near the city of Lagina, where Hekate was worshipped, and also a mountain called Nysa which was the birthplace of the god Dionysus.

Rather than princess Iambê telling her lewd jokes, in the Orphic version it was the old woman Baubo who made Demeter laugh by showing the goddess her genitals, and gave her kykeon. Baubo was also associated with Hekate as an alternative name or companion, as mentioned in the *Orphica*, and also on a defixio curse tablet from Claudiopolis, which linked Baubo/Hekate to Artemis and Ereschigal.[45] We may speculate as to whether the Baubo images of the woman displaying her genitalia re-appeared many centuries later in the medieval Sheela-na-gig figures found carved on churches around Europe.

In the telling of the *Homeric Hymn to Demeter*, Hekate embraced Persephone, and was described as being the *'preceder'* and *'follower'* of Persephone. This significantly referred to her position, not a role. Hekate preceded Persephone into the underworld and followed her out of the underworld. In this way she stood between her and any danger. Although Persephone assumed her role of chthonian Queen of the Dead during her third of the year in the underworld, for the other two thirds she was once again the gentle nurturing goddess walking the surface of the earth.

---

45 A Tabella Defixionis in the Museum of the University of Reading, Cormack, 1951

Persephone was in this aspect for her journeys to and from the underworld, and Hekate acted as her guardian as well as guide.

Demeter was strongly connected to Hekate, not only through the Eleusinian Mysteries, but at other Demeter temples where Hekate had a sanctuary and guarded the mysteries. Selinus on the island of Sicily was another Demeter and Persephone temple where Hekate was present at the gate, as was the temple on the island of Samothrace.

A scholiast on the *Argonautica* referred to Demeter (Deo) as Hekate's mother. This can be seen as another link in a curious chain of connections between Hekate, Demeter and Isis. Demeter was frequently syncretised with Isis, and then we see the subsequent syncretisation of Isis with Hekate. Hekate and Demeter meanwhile were connected through the Eleusinian Mysteries. Demeter and Isis and their myths were combined by the Greek historian Herodotus in the fifth century BCE (*Histories*), and continued to be so for many centuries, as can be seen from writers such as the Greek historian Diodorus Siculus (*Library of History*, first century BCE) and the Romano-Greek historian Plutarch (*Moralia*, second century CE).

A separate collection of material which may shed additional light on the mysteries of Eleusis is the Bacchic Gold Funeral Tablets of Orpheus, dating from the fifth century BCE to the second century CE. Amongst these funereal tablets created for Orphic initiates, we discover connections which emphasise the importance of Hekate at Eleusis, and the interconnection of the goddesses worshipped there. In the tablets Brimo, who was commonly identified as Hekate, was instead equated to both Demeter and Persephone, the other two goddesses of Eleusis.[46]

The second century CE Christian theologian Clement of Alexandria wrote of the Eleusinian Mysteries that, *"I fasted, I drank the kykeon."*[47] From this we know that the potential initiates would be in a receptive state due to fasting, which makes achieving altered states of consciousness easier. The role of the drink kykeon in the Eleusinian Mysteries is still the subject of much debate. From the Homeric Hymn we know that it was made from barley, water and pennyroyal. Pennyroyal is an abortificant, a fact which would have been known to the priestesses of Eleusis, who would have had skills in *pharmakeia*, the magic of herbs, drugs and poisons.

When barley gruel is mixed with water it starts to ferment, producing an alcoholic drink, a simple explanation which could account for an altered state of mind experienced by those drinking it, especially when combined with other herbs. One suggestion was that an ergot on the barley produced psychoactive effects; however this would have been both extremely difficult to control and potentially lethal.

It has also been suggested that opium was added to the kykeon, based on the amount of poppy imagery surrounding Demeter at Eleusis. This would certainly have had an effect on the initiate and put them into an altered state, but again we can only speculate. Alternatively an unknown psychoactive substance

---

46 Ritual Texts for the Afterlife, Graf & Johnston, 2007, p151.
47 Protrepticus, Clement of Alexander, C2nd CE, trans. H.R. Willoughby.

could have been added, such as psilocybin mushrooms, or indeed nothing at all. We do however know that kykeon as a drink was sought after for social gatherings, suggesting it obviously had some properties that made it desirable.

From depictions on vases showing Hekate with twin torches at the doorway to the sanctuary it seems likely that Hekate's role of *Propolos* was a key component of the initiations into the Eleusinian Mysteries. Thus Hekate priestesses may have guided the candidates through a network of underground caverns, lighting the way with the twin torches. Clement of Alexandria wrote describing a mystic drama taking place, and from his words it is clear he was referring to the myth of the abduction of Persephone, as described in the *Homeric Hymn to Demeter.*

> *"Deo [Demeter] and Kore became [the personages of] a mystic drama, and Eleusis with its dadouchos [torch-bearers, a title of Hekate] celebrates the wandering, the abduction, and the sorrow."*[48]

Another Christian writer, the African ex-pagan Lactantius, confirmed the role of the torch-bearing priestesses. He wrote in the fourth century CE, clearly referring to the drama, and said:

> *"With burning torches Proserpina [Persephone] is sought, and when she is found, the rite is closed with general thanksgiving and a waving of torches."*[49]

As mentioned above, Hekate was called *Dadouchos* ('*torch-bearer*'), whose light illuminated the path, hence her roles as *Phosphorus* ('*light-bringer*') and *Purphoros*

---

48 Protrepticus, Clement of Alexander, C2nd CE, trans. H.R. Willoughby.
49 Institutiones Divinae, Lactantius, C4th CE, trans. H.R. Willoughby.

('*fire-bringer*'). Reference was made to the role of her torches in an undated scholion saying of Hekate (with the god Apollo) that they *"fill the roads with light; he in the day, she in the night."* The fire of her torches would subsequently become the coiling stellar fire and intellectual fire of the *Chaldean Oracles*.

CHAPTER 4

IMAGES OF HEKATE

The oldest surviving image of Hekate is a small 20cm high terracotta statuette, from the sixth century BCE, depicting her crowned and enthroned in a pose which is similar to those commonly seen for the goddess Cybele, with whom she shared the title of *Brimo*.

The surviving ancient depictions of Hekate as three-formed were believed by the Greek geographer Pausanias to be copies of an earlier depiction by the sculptor Alkamenes. As Alkamenes was sculpting in the second half of the fifth century BCE, this indicated that the triple image was an early one, popularised by the famous sculpture known as the *Epipyrgidia* (*'on the tower'*) which stood near the statue of the wingless Nike (Victory):

> *"Of the gods, the Aiginetans worship most Hecate, in whose honour every year they celebrate mystic rites which, they say, Orpheus the Thracian established among them. Within the enclosure is a temple; its wooden image is the work of Myron, and it has one face and one body. It was Alkamenes, in my opinion, who first made three images of Hecate attached to one another, a figure called by the Athenians Epipyrgidia; it stands beside the temple of the Wingless Victory."*[50]

---

50 Description of Greece, Pausanias, C2nd CE, trans. J.G. Frazer.

A significant point made by Pausanias was the connection between Orpheus, and hence the Orphic Mysteries, and the mystic rites of Hekate. As we mentioned in the chapter on Eleusis, Hekate was a significant figure in the Orphic Mysteries, not least through her name of Brimo, which was recorded on Orphic Funeral Tablets as a password to be spoken by the initiate on death at the gates of the underworld to gain safe entry.

Another image of triple Hekate was carved on the Pergamon Frieze from the second century BCE. Hekate and Artemis battled the giants Klytios and Otios, with the triple Hekate wielding spear, torch, and shield. A dog belonging to one of the goddesses is seen biting the thigh of the giant Hekate attacked, who had serpents for legs.

Small triple shrines of Hekate were to be found outside the homes of those who honoured her. The name given to the small shrine was *hekataion.* The Greek comic playwright Aristophanes made reference to these in his play *The Wasps,* when one of the characters commented:

> *"I have heard it foretold, that one day the Athenians would dispense justice in their own houses, that each citizen would have himself a little tribunal constructed in his porch similar to the altars of Hecate."*[51]

As this play was written in 420 BCE, it shows that the worship of Hekate was widespread in the city of Athens by the late fifth century BCE. These triple statues would also be associated with crossroads, and Hekate *Trivia* (*'three ways'*).

---

51 The Wasps, Aristophanes, 420 BCE, trans. anon.

As well as being *Trimorphos* ('three-formed' or 'three-bodied'), she was also *Trioditis* ('of the three-ways' or 'of the crossroads'), a title which was also Latinized to *Trivia* (as *Trimorphos* was Latinized to *Triformis*). In this role she was the dreadful queen of the dead, attending the crossroads with her ghosts and *daimones*. In the Roman period when she was syncretised with Diana, that goddess also used the title and was called Diana *Trivia*.[52] Another title connected with this role was *Enodia* ('of the wayside' or 'of the crossroads'), which was originally the name of a Thessalian goddess who became assimilated into Hekate. This title was shared with Artemis, Selene and Persephone.

The earliest surviving images of Hekate at Eleusis also date to the fifth century BCE. These include the so-called *'Running Maiden'*, from around 480 BCE, which was originally attributed to Artemis, but has subsequently been identified as Hekate, bearing her characteristic two torches. A mid-fifth century BCE vase included an image of Hekate with her torches guarding the gate to the sanctuary, in her role as *Propylaia* ('the one before the gate').

The similarity in the way Hekate and Artemis were depicted at times has led to some confusion with images, as both goddesses were often shown in the same short *khiton* tunics, and with dogs. Artemis was sometimes portrayed with two torches, a more common Hekate attribute. Unless the figure had a bow and arrow or quiver of arrows, identifying her as Artemis, it could be difficult to say for certain, though the context

---

52 E.g. Hymn to Diana, Catullus, C1st BCE.

of companion figures made identification easier, e.g. Hermes would be more likely to be with Hekate than Artemis.

In later times, Eusebius, quoting Porphyry, gave a description of how a Hekate statute should be formed, which was said to come from the goddess herself:

> "Hecate also speaks of herself thus:
> 'Do all anon: a statue too therein;
> My form - Demeter bright with autumn fruits,
> White robes, and feet with golden sandals bound.
> Around the waist long snakes run to and fro,
> Gliding o'er all with undefiled track,
> And from the head down even to the feet
> Wrapping me fairly round with spiral coils.'
> And the material, she says, must be
> 'Of Parian stone or polish'd ivory.'"[53]

In his work *On Images*, Porphyry wrote of Hekate as the phases of the triple moon, which may have been the template for the idea of the witches' triple goddess that has been popularised since the mid-twentieth century:

> "But, again, the moon is Hecate, the symbol of her varying phases and of her power dependent on the phases. Wherefore her power appears in three forms, having as symbol of the new moon the figure in the white robe and golden sandals, and torches lighted: the basket, which she bears when she has mounted high, is the symbol of the cultivation of the crops, which she makes to grow up according to the increase of her light: and again the symbol of the full moon is the goddess of the brazen sandals."[54]

Eusebius, quoting Porphyry, added another element which reinforced this concept, when he

---

53 Praeparatio Evangelica, Eusebius, early C4th CE, trans. Des Places.
54 On Images, Porphyry, C3rd CE, trans. Taylor.

mentioned that the colours of white, red and black were associated with Hekate. These colours are the ones popularly associated with the witches' triple goddess:

> *"The symbols of Hecate are wax of three colours, white and black and red combined, having a figure of Hecate bearing a scourge, and torch, and sword, with a serpent to be coiled round her"*[55]

Another significant symbolism was that of her connection to the four elements. Hekate's connection to the four elements as a whole was emphasised in the sixth century CE by John Lydus in his work *Liber De Mensibus*:

> *"From whence they [the Chaldean tradition] hand down the mystical doctrine concerning the four elements and four-headed Hekate. For the fire-breathing head of a horse is clearly raised towards the sphere of fire, and the head of a bull, which snorts like some bellowing spirit, is raised towards the sphere of air; and the head of a hydra as being of a sharp and unstable nature is raised towards the sphere of water, and that of a dog as having a punishing and avenging nature is raised towards the sphere of earth."*[56]

Centuries earlier in the *Greek Magical Papyri*, Hekate was also referred to as *'four-faced'*, in the *Spell of Attraction*, which stated:

> *"Star-coursing, heavenly, torch-bearer, fire-breather, woman four-faced, four-named, four-roads' mistress."*[57]

Eusebius, again quoting Porphyry, wrote in the *Praeparatio Evangelica*, giving his detailed instructions

---

55 Praeparatio Evangelica, Eusebius, early C4th CE, trans. Des Places.
56 De Mensibus, Lydus, C6th CE, trans. Wunsch.
57 PGM IV.2559-60, trans. E.N. O'Neill.

which required the creation of incense using crushed lizards. The procedure was not overly complex and very practical, requiring a figure to be fashioned from rue and placed in a laurel shrine, after being censed with the special incense mixture which was made under the new moon.

> *"'That they themselves suggested how even their statues ought to be made, and of what kind of material, shall be shown by the response of Hecate in the following form:*
> *"My image purify, as I shall show:*
> *Of wild rue form the frame, and deck it o'er*
> *With lizards such as run about the house;*
> *These mix with resin, myrrh, and frankincense,*
> *Pound all together in the open air*
> *Under the crescent moon, and add this vow."*
> *'Then she set forth the vow, and showed how many lizards must be taken:*
> *"Take lizards many as my many forms,*
> *And do all this with care. My spacious house*
> *With branches of self-planted laurel form.*
> *Then to my image offer many a prayer,*
> *And in thy sleep thou shalt behold me nigh."*
> *'And again in another place she described an image of herself of this same kind.'"*[58]

It is interesting to note the use of rue in this structure, as rue was crushed in water with cedarwood used in the Babylonian ointment for anointing skulls and figurines used to communicate with ghosts, as described in the *Incantation to See a Ghost in Order to Make a Decision*.

This description was repeated by the German magician Cornelius Agrippa in his *De Occulta Philosophia* in 1533.[59] Several centuries later, in his

---

58 Praeparatio Evangelica, Eusebius, early C4th CE, trans. Des Places.
59 Of Occult Philosophy, Book 3, Agrippa, 1533.

Book of Witches (1908), Oliver Madox Hueffer gave a version of Porphyry's description, showing that interest was still extant in the early twentieth century. This was one of the few practical elements in Hueffer's book:

> "Make a wooden statue of the root of wild rue, well-polished, and anoint it with the bodies of little common lizards crushed into a paste with myrrh, storax and incense. Leave it in the open air during the waxing of the Moon and then (presumably at full Moon) speak as follows:- "Come infernal, terrestrial and celestial Bombo, Goddess of the highways and the cross-ways, enemy of the light who walkest abroad at night, friend and companion of the night, thou who delightest in the barking of dogs and in the shedding of blood, who wanderest amongst the shades and about the tombs, thou who desirest blood and who bringest terror unto the morals – Gorgo, Mormo, Moon of a thousand forms, cast a propitious eye upon our sacrifices." Then take as many lizards as Hecate has forms and fail not to make a grove of laurel boughs, the laurels having grown wild. Then, having addressed fervent prayers to the image, you will see her."[60]

Hueffer's representation of the process is interesting, as he mixed the process described by Eusebius, quoting Porphyry, with the chthonian invocation of Hekate given by Hippolytus:

> "Infernal and earthly and heavenly Bombo, come. Goddess of waysides, of cross-roads, lightbearer, nightwalker, Hater of the light, lover and companion of the night, Who rejoicest in the baying of hounds and in purple blood; Who dost stalk among corpses and the tombs of the dead Thirsty for blood, who bringest fear to mortals Gorgo and Mormo and Mene and many-formed one. Come thou propitious to our libations."[61]

---

60 The Book of Witches, p.145, Oliver Maddox Hueffer, 1908
61 Philosophumena or The Refutation of All Heresies, Hippolytus, C3rd CE, trans. Legge.

CHAPTER 5

VOCES MAGICAE

Voces magicae means *'magical words'*, and is a term used to refer to the apparently nonsensical words found in many spells in the *Greek Magical Papyri* and other texts.

Some of the words may be derived from older divine names, and one of the oldest and most significant sets of *voces magicae* was the *Ephesian Letters* or Characters, a group of six words. These words were *askion*, *kataskion*, *lix*, *tetrax*, *damnameneus* and *aision* (or *aisia*). We cannot be certain whether the Ephesian Letters were specifically connected with Hekate, though from the evidence it seems likely. Their first known appearance was in a Mycenaean inscription from the fifth century BCE:

> *"The Ephesian vengeance was sent down. Firstly Hecate harms the belongings of Megara in all things, and then Persephone reports to the gods. All these things are already so."*[62]

It is also significant that the first two of the Ephesian Letters were used in a Hekate charm in the *Greek Magical Papyri* (PGM LXX.12) as part of a string of *voces magicae*, being:

------

62 Stone inscription, Mycenae, late C5th BCE, trans. Jeffery.

"Askei Kataskei Eron Oreon Ior Mega Samnyer Baui Ohobantia Semne."

The third and fourth words, *Lix Tetrax*, appear in the second century Jewish proto-grimoire, the *Testament of Solomon* as the name of one of the demons summoned by the Jewish king. Curiously the name of the controlling angel for this demon was Azael, one of the fallen angels from the *Book of Enoch*.

The fifth word, *damnameneia*, was used in the *Bear Charm*, which included reference to Hekate as Brimo (PGM VII.686-702). An early fragmentary protective charm on a lead tablet from Phalasarna on Crete included the Ephesian Letters with phrases indicative of Hekate like 'She-wolf'. The connection between Hekate and *voces magicae* was further emphasised on an Egyptian lead tablet from the second or third century CE, which in its fragments included the reference:

> *"torches for Hecate Enodia; with a terrible voice the barbarously shouting goddess leads to the god"*[63]

The Ephesian Letters were also referred to by the Greek poet Anaxilas in the fourth century BCE, who wrote *"[unnamed person] carries around marvellous Ephesian letters in sewn pouches."*[64] Various qualities were attributed to the Ephesian Letters, including endowing the wearer with great power (particularly wrestlers as described in Eustathius, Photius and the Suda) and protecting newly married couples (mentioned by Menander, fragment 371).

---

63 Supplementum Magicum 49, Lead tablet, C2nd/3rd CE, trans. R.G. Edmonds III.
64 Fragment from his lost play The Harp Maker, C4th BCE, trans. R.G. Edmonds III.

It should also be noted that when Plutarch commented on the powers of the Ephesian Letters, he referred to daimones, who were specifically under the rule of Hekate:

> "For just as sorcerers advise those possessed by daimones to recite and name over to themselves the Ephesian letters."[65]

The Christian theologian Clement of Alexandria, who was well known for being the teacher of the theologian Origen, recorded suggested meanings for the Ephesian Letters in his work *Stromata* (*Miscellanies*) in the early third century CE:

> "Androkydes the Pythagorean, indeed, says that the so-called Ephesian letters, which were well-known among many, were of the order of symbols. And he said that Askion is darkness, for this has no shadow; and Kataskion is light, since it casts a shadow with its rays; and Lix is the earth, according to the ancient name; and Tetrax is the year, according to the seasons; and Damnameneus is the sun, the tamer; and Aisia is the true word. And truly the symbol signifies that the divine things have been set in order: darkness to light, the sun to the year, the earth to every kind of genesis of nature."[66]

The *voces magicae* increased in number and form in the subsequent centuries, and their descendants may be found in the so-called *barbarous words* encountered in the medieval grimoires. The *voces magicae* commonly contained at least one of the seven following formulae:

- Geometric Shapes – formed from the seven Greek vowels, commonly shaped into triangles, squares and *'wings'*.

---

65 Moralia 706E, Plutarch, early C2nd CE, trans. O'Neill.
66 Stromata V.8.43, Clement of Alexandria, early C3rd CE, trans. R.G. Edmonds III.

- Hebrew derived words – words ending in *–el* and *–oth*, which are terms associated with Hebrew divine names.
- Logoi – recurrent formulae of series of Voces Mysticae.
- Palindromes - such as the frequently used *Ablanathanalba*.
- Symbols - such as signs and seals and sometimes also known as charaktêres.
- *Voces Mysticae* – completely unrecognisable words.
- Vowel series – long strings of vowels, sometimes as Geometric Shapes.

Knowing that Hekate had a connection to witchcraft, a further remark which may reinforce the connection between her and *voces magicae* is found in the work of the Greek playwright Euripides. In his play *Iphigenia among the Taurians*, when Iphigenia prepared the sacrifice of Orestes, she *"shouted barbarous words, as a true witch"*.[67]

Significantly Iphigenia was associated with Hekate in *The Catalogue of Women* (eight-sixth century BCE), which has been attributed to Hesiod, author of the *Theogony*, though the date and authorship of the piece are disputed. Fragment 71, recorded by Pausanias, stated:

> *"I know that Hesiod in the 'Catalogue of Women' represented that Iphigenia [Iphimede] was not killed but, by the will of Artemis, became Hekate."*[68]

The third century CE theurgist Iamblichus, in a response to Porphyry, the Neoplatonic philosopher,

---

67 Iphigenia among the Taurians, Euripides, 414-412 BCE, trans H.G. Evelyn-White.
68 Pausanias's Description of Greece, Pausanias, C2nd CE, trans. J.G. Frazer.

stated clearly his beliefs regarding the importance of *voces magicae*:

> "But you ask, 'Why, of significant names, we prefer such as are Barbaric to our own?' ... we ought to think it necessary that our conference with the Gods should be in a language allied to them. Because likewise, such a mode of speech is the first and most ancient. And especially because those who first learned the names of the Gods, having mingled them with their own proper tongue, delivered them to us, that we might always preserve immoveable the sacred law of tradition, in a language peculiar and adapted to them."[69]

The use of *voces magicae* has continued through the centuries to the modern day, continuing a trend of confounding the mind with strange sounds, preparing it for the transformations that come during magical rites.

---

69 On the Mysteries of the Egyptians, Iamblichus, C3rd CE, trans T. Taylor.

CHAPTER 6

CHARMS FROM THE PGM

Charms and amulets were a regular occurrence in the ancient world. Such charms, with their instructions, revealed a great deal about the practices associated with this type of magic, as well as the specific deities and spiritual creatures referred to in them.

Hekate appeared on a number of amulets, including engraved gems, combined with Jewish divine names, usually in triple form. A particularly striking bronze triple Hekate amulet found at Ostia in Italy showed her bearing torches, daggers and scourges with King Solomon on the obverse side performing *hygromanteia* (demon summoning).

There are more references to Hekate in charms in the *Greek Magical Papyri* (PGM) than to any other goddess. Some of these references were to Hekate juxtaposed with other goddesses who became syncretised to her, such as Selene, Artemis, Persephone and Ereschigal. We have discussed these charms throughout the book where relevant, but in this chapter we give two diverse examples which demonstrate the range of material found in such charms.

List of Charms in the Greek Magical Papyri

For the benefit of the readers who may wish to follow up on them for their own satisfaction, we have included a précis of all the Hekate charms within the *Greek Magical Papyri*. This also includes significant examples of lead tablets of a similar nature which have references to Hekate on them.

Papyri	Purpose	Other Gods Mentioned	Notes
PGM III.1-64	Influencing the performance of a charioteer using the spirit of a cat, killed for the rite	Hermes, composite name of Hermekate	This charm is akin to a defixio, and uses lead lamellae
PGM IV.1390-1495	Love spell of attraction with the help of heroes, gladiators or other violently killed person	Anubis, Ereschigal, Hermes, Isis, Persephone Pluto, Zeus	Also uses Hebrew divine names
PGM IV.2006-2125	Pitys spell of attraction to draw desired thing (not specifically a love or sex spell)	Osiris	Three-formed Hekate drawn on flax leaf with cow, maiden and dog heads
PGM IV.2241-2358	Spell to the waning moon	Hermes, Mene, Michael (archangel), Osiris, Persephone (Kore)	Long sequence of voces magicae

PGM IV.2441-2621	Spell of attraction, also for causing illness, destroying, sending dreams and dream revelations	Aphrodite, Artemis, Ereschigal, Hermes, Persephone, Selene	Three distinct coercive spells with voces magicae
PGM IV.2622-2707	Slander spell to Selene, for attraction, dreams, causing sickness, removing enemies, protection	Selene	Charm is made by engraving Hekate on a magnetite heart
PGM IV.2708-84	Love spell of attraction	Artemis, Ereschigal, Persephone (Kore), Selene	Offering made in an earthenware censer on a lofty rooftop on the 13th or 14th
PGM IV.2785-2890	Prayer to Selene for any spell	Artemis, Mene, Persephone, Selene	Charm made from lodestone with three-formed Hekate with dog, horned maiden and goat heads
PGM IV.2943-66	Love spell of attraction through wakefulness		Dog figure made with bat's eyes and left at crossroads
PGM VII.686-702	Bear charm	Artemis	Includes the fifth Ephesian Letter
PGM VII.756-94	Prayer	Mene	Includes list of signs and symbols

PGM VII.862-918	Lunar spell of Claudianus	Ereschigal, Selene	Includes twelve angels of the hours
PGM XXXVI.187-210	Love spell of attraction		Also uses Hebrew divine names and square of Greek vowels
PGM LXX.4-25	Charm of Hekate Ereschigal against fear of punishment	Ereschigal	Includes first two Ephesian Letters
PGM CXIV.1-14	Charm against epilepsy		Fragmentary charm
PGM CXXIII a-f	Medical charms	Thoth (dog-headed baboon)	Hebrew names and angels
Phalasarna, Crete, C4th BCE	Protection spell	Apollo, Herakles, Nike, Zeus	Fragmentary charm, includes the Ephesian Letters
Egypt, C2nd-3rd CE Supplementum Magicum 49	Love spell	Aion, Aphrodite, Artemis, Nyx, Erebus, Persephone	Fragmentary charm, includes list of signs and symbols

Symbols from the PGM

Several of the spells in the Greek Magical Papyri have lists of symbols given for the summoning of Hekate's aid. To demonstrate the frequency of these symbols they are given below. We have also included in this list the symbols mentioned in a Hekate charm found in the magical papyri from the same period gathered in *Supplementum Magicum 49*.

Table of Items in Hekate Symbol Lists

Symbol Item	PGM IV.2334-38	PGM VII.780-85	PGM LXX. 4-25	Supplementum Magicum 49
Virgin		X	X	
Black dog/Bitch	X	X	X	X
Serpent			X	X
Garland/Wreath		X	X	
Key	X	X	X	X
Wand/Herald's Wand	X	X	X	X
Golden Sandal			X	X
Bronze Sandal	X			X

Bear Charm

The flavour of this charm resembled the role of Hekate in the *Chaldean Oracles* as the world soul and dispositer of divine actions. This charm was one of those with Artemis and Hekate combined. A number of titles of Artemis were seen, such as *'chief huntress'*, *'shooter of deer'*, *'Taurian'*. Likewise names associated with Hekate, such as Brimo and Baubo were also seen, and titles which could indicate her, like *'earth-breaker'*, recalling her title of *Nexichthon* (*'she who breaks open the earth'*), as well as the fifth of the Ephesian Letters, *Damnameneia*:

> Bear, Bear, you who rule the heaven, the stars, and the whole world; you who make the axis turn and control the whole cosmic system by force and compulsion; I appeal to you, imploring and supplicating that you may do the NN thing, because I call upon you with your holy names at which your deity rejoices, names which you are not able to ignore: Brimo, earth-breaker, chief huntress, Baubo L ... I Aumor Amor Amor ... Iea [shooter] of deer Amam[amar] Aphrou ... Ma, universal queen, queen of wishes, Amama, well-bedded, Dardanian, all-seeing, night-running, man-attacker, man-subduer, man-summoner, man-conqueror, Lichrissa Phaessa, O aerial one, O strong one, O song and dance, guard, spy, delight, protector, adamant, adamantine, O Damnameneia Brexerikandara, most high, Taurian, unutterable, fire-bodied, light-giving, sharply armed. Do such-and-such things. [70]

---

70 PGM VII.686-702, trans. H.D. Betz.

Charm of Hekate Ereschigal

The rubric for this charm actually contained three different intentions, namely (1) protection in the underworld, (2) receiving the answer to a question in a dream, and (3) disruption of another person's sleep. It is also worth noting that the first sequence of *voces magicae* started with the first two of the Ephesian Letters.

The charm begins with a declaration that no harm can affect the speaker, who identifies with Ereschigal (and is therefore female) and who is holding her thumbs. Holding thumbs was an apotropaic (*'evil-averting'*) gesture in the ancient world.

The speaker is then advised that if the being in question (who logically would be a denizen of the underworld) comes close, to take hold of the right heel (another apotropaic gesture) and recite a list of Hekate symbols which deflects him. The list contains the words Ereschigal, virgin, bitch, serpent, wreath, key, herald's wand, golden sandal of the Lady of Tartaros (see previous table for a comparison with other such lists).

The speaker then recites a list of *voces magicae* and makes a significant declaration at the crossroads before turning and fleeing (a standard practice when you wanted Hekate's aid but did not want to encounter her):

> *"Askei Kataskei Erōn Oreōn Iōr Mega Samnyēr Baui (3 times) Phobantia Semnē, I have been initiated, and I went down into the [underground] chamber of the*

Dactyls, and I saw the other things down below, virgin, bitch, and all the rest."[71]

If the charm was spoken late at night it would reveal the answer to a question during sleep, and for someone being led to death, if said while scattering sesame seeds it would save them. A second list of *voces magicae* was included for the final part of the charm:

'*Phorba Phorba Brimo Azziebya*'

The charm continued with instructions for the practitioner to make a cake from the best quality bran, sandalwood and sharp vinegar. Onto this cake the name of the recipient was inscribed with a request to take away his sleep.

---

71 PGM LXX.4-25, trans. H.D. Betz.

CHAPTER 7

CHARMS FOR LOVE

When a person resorts to love magic, the likelihood is that it will not be for a pure and noble motive. This phenomenon has occurred for thousands of years and will probably continue to do so. In the ancient Greek world love magic was usually either performed to bind or punish an unfaithful lover, or break up a relationship to try and win someone's partner, or to make oneself irresistible to members of the opposite (or same) sex. Thus in the following request, where Hekate was addressed by the title of *Kourotrophos*, an older man asked the goddess to direct a younger woman's attention in his direction:

> *"Hear me as I pray Kourotrophos. Grant that this woman may refuse the affection and bed of young men, but let her find joy in old men with wizened temples, whose strength is blunted but whose desire remains keen."*[72]

Faraone suggested in *Ancient Greek Love Magic* (1999) that the popularity of underworld deities like Hermes and Hekate with her daimones and ghosts for love magic became dominant from around the first century BCE. Prior to this Aphrodite and her entourage, and Selene the Moon and Helios the Sun had also been commonly invoked for love spells.

---

72 Life of Homer, Herodotus, C5th BCE, trans. Faraone.

Speaking of Hekate's association with this kind of love magic from this latter period he observed:

> "It is this last form, with its nocturnal graveside ceremonies, that endures in later antiquity and forms the slim factual core for the popular caricature that we find in Roman poetry of ugly hags digging up corpses with their bare hands and uttering barbarous and frightening incantations."[73]

However this does ignore the fact that the single largest group of spells invoking Hekate in the *Greek Magical Papyri* are love spells. Although the time period of the *Greek Magical Papyri* is later, from the second century BCE to the fifth century CE, nevertheless the portrayal of Hekate within them is not the hag and corpse image, rather it is the triple-headed and animal-headed goddess who became syncretised with other goddesses such as Selene, Artemis and Persephone.

Looking at the content of the spells, we can see that they expressed several of the themes found associated with Hekate's rites. Thus one love spell of attraction used the help of the ghosts of the untimely dead through the use of grave dirt, and another used incense in an earthen censer. A third spell used a combination of magical techniques, including a magical ring and a simulacrum of a dog with eyes from a live bat.

In the *"Love Spell of attraction performed with the help of heroes or gladiators or those who have died a violent death."*[74] a piece of bread from a loaf which was being eaten was broken into seven bite-sized pieces

---

73 Ancient Greek Love Magic, Faraone, 1999.
74 PGM IV.1390-1495, trans. E.N. O'Neill.

and taken to the location of the violent death, and thrown to the ground with the words of the spell. Earth from the ground where the death occurred and the bread had been thrown, was removed and thrown inside the house of the woman who was desired. The chthonian powers were invoked in force, with Hekate, Hermes and Kore all petitioned, as well as the Roman Pluto and Egyptian Anubis, and the ghosts of the untimely dead, to torment the woman until she succumbed to the spell-caster. This was repeated for three days, and if it failed a further spell cast over dung from a black cow offered on ashes of flax, with the dirt being cast again.

By contrast, *"Another love spell of attraction."*[75] used the offering of incense, and was described as an offering to Selene, though from the rubric it is obvious that Hekate was the focus of the spell. Ethiopian cumin and fat from a dappled virgin goat were burned in an earthen censer on a lofty housetop (i.e. closer to the sky) on the 13th or 14th day of the month. This dating implied a full moon, referring to the 13th and 14th day of the lunar cycle.

A further love spell required a bronze stylus, which was frequently used for engraving on pottery and lead, emphasising the sacred metal of Hekate. This spell not only used *voces magicae* but also included Hebrew and Gnostic divine names. The identification at the end of the spell with Synkoutouel was probably with an angel, indicated by the *–el* ending of the name. Significantly Hekate was called on three-formed, and the person

---

75 PGM IV.2708-84.

declared they were holding two serpents in their right hand.[76]

The *"Love-spell of attraction through wakefulness"*[77] was the sort of spell which might make a modern reader squirm, but would not have been seen as anything out of the ordinary in the ancient world. The spell required the eyes of a live bat to be removed and placed in the figure of a dog made from unbaked dough or unmelted wax. This was placed in a new drinking vessel with the papyrus strip containing the spell rubric attached to it, sealed with a ring with crocodile heads on (symbolising the Egyptian crocodile god Sobek) and the whole deposited at a crossroads. Hekate was also equated with Kore (Persephone) in the rubric of the spell.

By far the best example of a binding spell from ancient Greece is found in the *Idylls* of the Greek poet Theocritus, circa 270 BCE. A spurned lover who was obviously a proficient sorceress worked her magic against the foolish man who betrayed her, effectively giving us a catalogue of many of the practices used at the time. We may note the juxtaposition of Hekate with Selene, demonstrating that this assimilation of the moon goddess by Hekate was already occurring at this time. Much of the piece described the feelings of the spurned woman (and has been omitted here), but where techniques were used clear insights have been provided:

> *"Where are my bay leaves? Bring them, Thestylis! Where are my love charms? Tie a thread of fine crimson wool around the bowl that I may work a spell*

---

76 PGM XXXVI.187-201.
77 PGM IV.2943-66.

to bind my lover who is so cruel to me ... But now I bind him with a fire spell. Shine brightly, sweet Moon; I will chant softly to you, Goddess, and to infernal Hekate – before whom the dogs shiver when she wanders over the graves of the dead where the dark blood lies. Hail to thee, dreadful Hekate, and stay with me to the end; make these drugs as potent as those of Circe and Medea and golden-haired Perimede.

Draw my lover here, iynx.

First, the barley grains must burn on the fire. Throw them on, Thestylis ... Throw them on and say: 'These are Delphis' bones I throw on.'

Draw my lover here, iynx.

Delphis brought me pain, and so I burn this bay leaf against Delphis. As it crackles in the flames with a sharp noise and flares leaving no trace of ash, so may Delphis' body melt in the flame.

Draw my lover here, iynx.

Now I burn the corn husks. Artemis, you have the power to move even the steel in Hades or anything else that is unmovable ... Thestylis, the dogs are howling around town: the Goddess is at the crossroads. Quick, bang the gong!

Draw my lover here, iynx.

As I melt this wax with Hekate's help, so may Delphis of Myndus melt immediately from love. And as this bronze rhombus whirls by the grace of Aphrodite, so may he whirl at my door.

Draw my lover here, iynx.

Three times I pour a libation, mighty Goddess, and three times do I say: 'whether it is a woman or a man who lies with him now, may he forget them as quickly as Theseus once in Dia, forgot lovely-haired Ariadne.'

Draw my lover here, iynx.

Coltsfoot is an Arcadian herb, that makes all the fillies and the swift mares run madly in the hills. May I see Delphis in such a state, coming to my door raving like a madman from the oil of the wrestling school.

Draw my lover here, iynx.

Delphis lost this fringe from his coat: now I shred it and cast it into the ravenous flames...

Draw my lover here, iynx.
I shall crush a lizard tomorrow and bring him an evil
drink. Thestylis, take these magic herbs and smear
them on his threshold while it is still dark, and
spitting say: 'I smear the bones of Delphis.'
Draw my lover here, iynx.
...

Now shall I bind him with my love magic, but if he
still causes me pain, he shall beat on the gate of
Hades, such evil drugs, I keep for him in my box;
Goddess, it is something I learned from an Assyrian
stranger."[78]

More than two hundred years later, Virgil adapted this spell given by Theocritus, in his *Eclogue 8, The Sorceress.*[79] Maintaining the style and much of the technique, Virgil removed references to Hekate, changed the name of the protagonist from Delphis to Daphnis, and made the herb supplier a werewolf, emphasising the malefic nature of the magic.

---

78 Idylls 2, Theocritus, 270BCE, trans. Z. Yardley.
79 Eclogues, Virgil, c.40 BCE.

CHAPTER 8

DEFIXIONES

A type of binding spells known as *defixiones*, were used from the fifth century BCE through to at least the fourth century CE and beyond. The term is derived from the Latin word *defixio*, meaning *'to nail down'* or *'transfix'*. Defixiones, when invoking the aid of a deity, almost always called on chthonic deities including Hekate, along with Hermes, Ge, Persephone and Hades.

Defixiones were usually inscribed onto a lead tablet, and folded up and pierced with one (or several) bronze or iron nails. They were commonly placed in with the corpse of someone who had died suddenly or in chthonic sanctuaries, and in later periods in bodies of water such as baths, wells and springs. Hekate's association with both the untimely dead, who it was believed frequently remained earthbound as ghosts, and the magical associations of bronze as her sacred metal further emphasised the connection between her and defixiones.

The connection between defixiones and the dead continued the Egyptian practice of Letters to the Dead, which date back as far as 3100 BCE, and were often regarding the same themes, such as assistance with love or legal matters. The ancient Egyptians believed that the dead had more magical power than the living and could be enlisted for their aid. Those who died a violent death or died young were particularly regarded as being good assistants, a practice which continued into Greek magic.

The *Greek Magical Papyri* gave detailed instructions for the creation of defixiones, which although they have a late date of third-fourth century CE, illustrated clearly the principles involved.[80] There is no reason to assume that the techniques described changed in any major way over the previous centuries, except the emphasis on lead tablets as the basis for writing the curse onto.

The sequence of practices to create and use a defixio was not complex, which may be one reason for the popularity of the technique. A lead lamella or piece of papyrus was used as the basis for the defixio. If it was a lead lamella, the words of the binding curse was written on it with a stylus, usually made of bronze. The lead lamellae was then folded in half, and pierced with a bronze or iron nail all the way through.

For papyrus, myrrh ink was used to draw around an iron ring inside and out to mark two circles. The words and any characters were then written inside the circles, and the ring placed back on the papyrus in the same place. The papyrus was wrapped around the ring and the pen or a nail used to pierce the centre of the ring.

The defixio, whatever it was made of, would then be either buried in the grave of someone who died in an untimely fashion (i.e. the restless dead), or thrown into a water source such as a well or lake. In either case the defixio was seen as being moved more into the

---

80 PGM V.304-337.

realm of the underworld, where the chthonic deities like Hekate, or her ghosts and daimones could carry out the requests made on it.

Defixiones can be divided into four categories, these being direct-binding, prayer formula, wish formula and analogy formula, of which only one concerns us as being used with Hekate. This formula is the prayer formula, where a god or daimon was invoked and encouraged to bind a person, e.g. *Restrain [Name]*. As mentioned above Hekate, along with Hermes, Ge, Persephone and Hades, was one of the most common deities found invoked on the defixiones.

The curses themselves found on the defixiones may be further divided into five categories, athletic or theatrical binding of rivals, binding charioteers or gladiators (from the second century CE), binding a love rival, binding a lover's desires, and judicial binding to win court cases. The latter category was one of the most popular, and often called on Hekate, so we see examples where the person was bound, along with any legal advocates or witnesses for them. Hekate Chthonia and Hermes Chthonia as a pair were often called on for such defixiones.[81]

On rare occasions Hekate was referred to without using her name, such as in a fourth century BCE lover binding defixio from a grave, which began *"I bind Theodora in the presence of the one [female] at Persephone's side and in the presence of those who are unmarried."*[82] Here Hekate was being described in her role as *Propolos*, or companion to Persephone in her journey to and from the underworld.

---

81 E.g. Doric defixio, late fifth-early fourth century BCE.
82 Attic defixio, fourth century BCE, trans. J. Gager.

Occasionally a defixio was purely motivated by jealousy of position or wealth, as this third century example found in a tomb seems to be. This example is interesting in that it used a formula found in Book VIII of Homer's *Illiad* and also in Hesiod's *Theogony*, that of binding in murky Tartarus:

> *"I will bind Sôsikleia and her property and great fame and fortune and mind. Let her become hateful to friends. I will bind her under murky Tartarus in troublesome bonds, with Hekate Chthonios."*[83]

An unusual defixio from the first century CE was found in a well in the Agora in Athens. It was unusual in the tone, as the person who commissioned the defixio specified exceptions to the curse for an unwilling accomplice. The associated image was unique, and was originally described as *"a figure of a bat with outspread wings"*! Subsequently it has been described as a six-armed Hekate, and clearly the image is triple-headed, and bears torches in the upper pair of arms, with the lower pair being distinctly serpentine. The wheel and eight-rayed symbol on this defixio both also appeared in a bronze triple Hekate amulet found at Ostia in Italy, with King Solomon on the obverse side performing *hygromanteia* (demon summoning).

The long defixio referred to Hekate with multiple titles such as Chthonia, Trioditis, triple-faced, single-faced, of the heavens, and asked her to wield her bronze sickle and cut them (the criminals) out.[84]

A later defixio from the third century CE again linked Hekate with other chthonian deities, i.e. Hermes, Pluto, and Kore (identified with the

---

83 Attic defixio, third century BCE, trans. J. Gager.
84 Athenian Defixio, first century CE, trans. J. Gager.

Babylonian Ereschigal). It was incomplete and appeared to be a binding spell for a homosexual love affair. Hekate was the dominant deity in the defixio, and it also contained a large number of *voces magicae*. One section, for instance, reads:

> *"I call upon you, mistress ruler of all mankind, all-dreadful one, bursting out of the earth, who also gathers up the limbs of Meliouchos and Meliouchos[85] himself, Ereschigal Neboutosoualêth Erebennê Arkuia Nekui Hekate, true Hekate, come and accomplish for me this very act!"[86]*

A defixio from Asia Minor again linked Hekate as Baubo, with other deities, specifically Artemis and Ereschigal, and interestingly it also mentioned angels:

> *"Ortho (Artemis), Baubo (Hekate), ... Ereschigal, ... sovereign gods and angels, bind with your spell all those herein written."[87]*

The popularity of defixiones, with curses or binding spells written onto leads tablets persisted long into the Renaissance, with engraved lead plates being used with demons to force thieves to return stolen property in the seventeenth century CE.

---

85 Meliouchos occurs in a number of the Greek Magical Papyri, and may be a name for the Egyptian god Osiris.
86 Alexandrian Defixio, third century CE, trans. J. Gager.
87 A Tabella Defixionis in the Museum of the University of Reading, Cormack, 1951

CHAPTER 9

THE ARMOUR OF HEKATE

The *Chaldean Oracles* provided a significant practical piece of ritual technique to be used by the theurgist to prepare himself. Essentially it was to visualise armour of light onto yourself prior to magical work. In modern times, this technique of praying on armour of light is one which has been adopted by elements within the Christian church as part of their struggle for religious supremacy against the forces of darkness (as they see them) that oppose them. The theurgist was advised:

> *"Having put on the complete-armed vigour of resounding light.*
> *With triple strength fortifying the soul and the mind,*
> *He must put into the mind the symbol of variety, and not walk dispersedly on the empyreal channels, but collectively.*
> *For being furnished with every kind of armour, and armed, he is similar to the goddess."*[88]

When suitably armoured the theurgist would be similarly prepared to the goddess, as indicated by another fragment of the *Chaldean Oracles*, where Hekate stated:

> *"For I have come, a goddess in full armour and with weapons."*[89]

---

88 Proclus commentary on Plato's Timaeus, C5th CE, trans. Taylor.
89 Chaldean Oracles, C2nd CE, trans. Johnston.

An earlier and more physical example of magical armour was given in the tale of the Golden Fleece. Medea created the magical ointment for Jason, which made him invulnerable when rubbed into his armour and skin. Symbolically we may see a precedent here, with the hero who has the grace of Hekate being granted temporary invulnerability, a state which soon wears out (after a day), as does the love of the fickle hero.

This idea finds a parallel in the Kabbalistic practice of strengthening the subtle body by praying the Hebrew letters over the different parts of the body. When this practice was first used and whether the techniques cross-fertilised each other is impossible to say, though we may note that the second century CE Kabbalistic text, the *Sepher Yetzirah* (*'Book of Formation'*) detailed the body parts corresponding to all the letters of the Hebrew alphabet.

CHAPTER 10

GLIMPSES OF INITIATION

An intriguing reference in one of the *Greek Magical Papyri* from the third or fourth century CE may hint at the survival of an initiation ritual connected with Hekate. The subterranean setting is appropriate, as may be seen from initiation ceremonies from other mysteries such as Eleusis:

> "'Askei Kataskei Erōn Oreōn Iōr Mega Samnyēr Baui (3 times) Phobantia Semnē, I have been initiated, and I went down into the [underground] chamber of the Dactyls, and I saw the other things down below, virgin, bitch, and all the rest.' ... and if you are led away to death, say it while scattering seeds of sesame, and it will save you."[90]

The combination of the first two words of the Ephesian Letters (*Askei Kataskei*) with the reference to seeing *"things down below, virgin, bitch"* clearly hinted at Hekate's involvement in the process. Hekate would be the virgin, and the bitch would be the black dog which accompanies her.

The reference to sesame seeds is also significant, for this was one of the ingredients in the *kalathoi*, the offerings made in the Eleusinian Mysteries.

The Dactyls were said to be born of the earth goddess Rhea, and to be magicians who invented iron-working. They protected the baby Zeus from his father

---

90 PGM LXX.4-25, trans. H.D. Betz.

Cronos by banging their weapons and making noise, covering his cries from the cave he was hidden in.

We know from writings about Samothrace that there were initiation rites celebrated there and that they took place in caves, as recorded in the tenth century CE Byzantine encyclopaedia the *Suda*, from unknown sources:

> *"In Samothrace there were certain initiation-rites, which they supposed efficacious as a charm against certain dangers. In that place were also the mysteries of the Corybantes and those of Hecate and the Zerinthian cave, where they sacrificed dogs"*[91]

Whether these were the same rites hinted at in the *Greek Magical Papyri* we cannot be certain. The Greek poet Nonnus also obliquely mentioned the rites of Samothrace in his classic work *Dionysiaca*:

> *"[The Kabeiros] Alkon grasped a fiery bolt in one hand, and swung about a festal torch of Hekate from his own country [i.e. Samothrace]."*[92]

Hekate was also worshipped with a mystery cult on the island of Aigina, with Pausanias writing:

> *"of the gods, the Aiginetans honour Hekate the most and they celebrate her mystery every year, saying Orpheus of Thrace established it for them. Inside the enclosure is a temple with a wooden statue by Myron having one face and body."*[93]

Myron was a famous Athenian sculptor, who worked mainly in bronze, during the period 480-440 BCE, making the temple image of Hekate contemporary with Alkamenes famous three-formed image of Hekate. The mention of Orpheus is also significant, for the

---

91 Suda, Alpha 1164, C10th CE, trans. J. Benedict.
92 Dionysiaca 29.213, Nonnus, C5th CE, trans. W.H.D. Rouse.
93 Pausanias's Description of Greece, Pausanias, C2nd CE, trans. J.G. Frazer.

Orphic Mysteries incorporated the Homeric Hymn to Demeter, with Hekate being a significant part of that myth. They were also vegetarians who believed in the transmigration of the soul (reincarnation). Whether such themes from the Orphic Mysteries would have been included in the mysteries of Hekate at Aigina we can only speculate.

Referring to the mysteries of Hekate at Aigina in which her husband was an initiate, the Roman priestess Paulina wrote in the fourth century CE:

> *"You instruct me as minister of Hecate in the triple secret."*[94]

This intriguing comment does not give much away, although the reference to the *'triple secret'* does hint at Hekate Triformis, and also recalls the extensive use of triplicity in her rites.

---

94 Tomb inscription by Paulina to her husband Vettius Agorius Praetextatus, 384 CE, trans. M.R. Lefkowitz.

CHAPTER 11

HERBS & POISONS

Hekate was often referred to as being closely associated with plants of death, such as poisonous herbs and funereal plants. Likewise her priestesses (or daughters) Medea and Circe were particularly associated with *pharmakeia*, the magic of herbs, drugs and poisons. However despite long lists presented in many modern pagan works, there is little historical evidence from ancient Greece and Rome beyond what is given below of connections between Hekate and specific plants. Many modern attributions seem to be plants connected with death or having psychoactive properties (the so-called hexing herbs). This does not invalidate the connection, it merely makes it a recent addition rather than one with an ancient provenance.

Many herbs and plants were mentioned in the *Orphic Argonautica* as growing in Hekate's garden. We have only included entries on these if there are other references elsewhere, to ensure there was a connection rather than it simply being poetic license:

"In the furthest recesses of the enclosure was a sacred grove, shaded by flourishing trees. In it there were many laurels and cornels and tall plane trees. Within this the grass was carpeted with low-growing plants with powerful roots. Famous asphodel, pretty maidenhair, rushes, galangal, delicate verbena, sage, hedge-mustard, purple honeysuckle, healing cassidony, flourishing field basil, mandrake, hulwort, in addition fluffy dittany, fragrant saffron, nose-

smart, there too lion-foot, greenbrier, camomile, black poppy, alcua, all-heal, white hellebore, aconite, and many other noxious plants grew from the earth. In the middle a stout oak tree with heaven-high trunk spread its branches out over much of the grove. On it hung, spread out over a long branch, the golden fleece, over which watched a terrible snake."[95]

Aconite

One of the best known herbs associated with Hekate was aconite (also known as monkshood or wolfbane). Diodorus Siculus wrote that it was discovered by Hekate and tested on strangers to discover the dosage.[96] He attributed mortal origins to Hekate, though he also described her as the mother of Circe and Medea. It was believed that aconite was formed by the saliva which fell to the earth from the mouths of the triple-headed hell-hound Cerberus when he was dragged into the daylight by the demi-god Hercules.

Ebony

We may suggest the black wood of ebony as being associated with Hekate from the thrice-folding doors of ebony which gave access to her garden. Ebony was particularly associated with the underworld, and Hermes Chthonia. Reference was made to this in the *Greek Magical Papyri*, where it observed, *"I also know your wood: ebony."*[97]

---

95 Orphic Argonautica, C4th CE, trans. D. Ogden.
96 Library of History 45.4.2-3, Diodorus Siculus, C1st BCE, trans. Oldfather.
97 PGM VIII.13.

Garlic

Garlic was one of the substances offered to Hekate at the *deipnon* (Hekate supper). Garlic had a reputation from ancient Egypt as an apotropaic plant providing protection from the restless dead. The Greek naturalist Theophrastus made reference to garlic at the crossroads in his *Characters* where he described the *Superstitious Man* as one who would:

> *"if ever he observes anyone feasting on the garlic at the cross-roads, he will go away, pour water over his head, and, summoning the priestesses, bid them carry a squill or a puppy around him for purification"*[98]

Mandrake

The presence of mandrake in Hekate's garden in the *Orphic Argonautica* was not surprising. Theophrastus wrote in *Enquiry into Plants* in the fourth century BCE about drawing three circles around the mandrake with an iron sword before picking it, recalling the contemporary practices of necromantic and chthonic rites.

The Jewish historian Flavius Josephus wrote in the first century CE about mandrake, and was the first person to postulate the use of a dog to pull the root out. This was the origin of the idea of the dog dying from the scream of the mandrake.

> *"They dig all around it [the mandrake], leaving but a minute portion of the root covered; they then tie a dog to it, and the animal rushing to follow the person who tied him, easily pulls it up, but instantly dies – a*

---

98 The Superstitious Man, Characters, C4th BCE, trans. Jebb.

vicarious victim, as it were, for him who intended to remove the plant."⁹⁹

The sacrifice of the dog to gain the root, (which was known as *baara*,) used in demon-expelling rings[100] for dealing with possession, holds clear echoes of Hekate's powers and associations.   The demon-expelling mandrake-holding ring was specifically associated with Solomon, and was described as being made of iron and brass (another copper-based alloy like bronze, and often used as an alternative name for bronze).   A consequence of this connection with Hekate may have been the medieval belief that mandrake was most powerful if gathered at the crossroads.

Oak

Hekate was referred to on more than one occasion in connection with serpents and oak leaves, so it is possible this plant may have been sacred to her (as well as to Zeus).   The fifth century BCE Greek tragedian Sophocles described her thus in *The Root-Cutters*, saying:

> *"She who is crowned with oak-leaves*
> *And the coils of wild serpents."[101]*

This may well have inspired the reference in Apollodorus' *Argonautica*, when Jason conjures Hekate using the methods taught him by Medea, and:

> *"the dread goddess, from the uttermost depths and came to the sacrifice of Aeson's son; and round her*

---

99 The Jewish War, Flavius Josephus, C1st CE, trans. S.S. Kottek,
100 Jewish Antiquities, Flavius Josephus, C1st CE, trans. W. Whiston.
101 The Root-Cutters, Sophocles, C5th BCE, trans. Z. Yardley.

horrible serpents twined themselves among the oak boughs."[102]

Further there is an oak tree in the centre of Hekate's garden in the *Orphic Argonautica*, on which hung the Golden Fleece and its guardian serpent, maintaining the connection between the tree and the serpent.

Saffron

Saffron was associated with both Hekate and her cousin Artemis (at her temple at Brauron). In the *Orphic Hymn to Hekate*, she was described as *"saffron-cloaked goddess of the heavens."[103]* The *Orphic Argonautica* also listed saffron as one of the plants in Hekate's garden. The phrase *"saffron-dyed"* was used three times in PGM CXXIII, in sections a, e and f. A number of the titles in the charms are ones that were used for Hekate. The name Brimo was also used twice in the associated images with the charms.

Yew

Yew is often described as sacred to Hekate, though there is little evidence to support this in the texts beyond a reference in the *Thebaid* of Statius:

> *"Let her lead them with torches of flaming yew; let her give three swings of her mighty serpent; and do not let the heads of Cerberus be obstacles to those deprived of light."[104]*

---

102 Argonautica, Book 3, Apollonius, C3rd CE, trans. R.C. Seaton.
103 Orphic Hymn to Hekate, C1st-3rd CE, trans. Z. Yardley.
104 Thebaid, Statius, C1st CE, trans. C.S. Ross.

This association between Hekate and the yew probably stems from the long association between the yew and death, as witnessed by the reference in the *Aeneid*, when Queen Dido was preparing for her suicide:

> *"Sad cypress, vervain, yew, compose the wreath,*
> *And ev'ry baleful green denoting death."*[105]

The connection between Hekate and the yew tree was emphasised by Shakespeare in *Macbeth*, and this has probably stuck, when Hekate said to the witches:

> *"With new fallen dew from churchyard yew, I will but*
> *'noint and then I'll mount."*[106]

Additionally there was the reference made to the *"slips of yew, silvered in the moon's eclipse"*[107] thrown into the cauldron by the witches in the famous cauldron scene of the play.

Unspecified Herbs

Both Circe and Medea were famous for their legendary skills with herbs. Circe used her knowledge of herbs, said to have been gained from Hekate, to punish and transform those who crossed her. This is seen in the story told of her actions when Glaucus chose the maiden Scylla over her. Circe transformed Scylla into a hideous monster after Glaucus boasted he would love her no matter what happened:

> *"She made a brew of herbs, and as she cooked them*
> *She sang aloud songs learned from Hecate –*
> *Singing that should make any mortal tremble."*[108]

---

105 The Aeneid, Virgil, late C1st BCE, trans. John Dryden.
106 Macbeth, Shakespeare, c.1606 CE.
107 Macbeth, Shakespeare, c.1606 CE.
108 Metamorphoses, Ovid, 8CE, trans. Gregory.

Medea also used her knowledge for revenge, poisoning the wedding dress for Creusa, the young bride chosen by Jason over her:

> *"My prayers are heard: thrice has bold Hecate bayed loud, and has raised the accursèd fire with its baleful light. Now all my power is marshalled; hither call my sons that by their hands thou mayst send these costly gifts unto the bride."[109]*

Other female figures were happy to take advantage of the magical and poisonous herbs associated with Hekate. The goddess Athena used magical herbs to transform the boastful maiden Arachne into a spider following her loss of the weaving contest between the two of them:

> *"And as she turned away she sprayed her features With droppings from dark herbs of Hecate;"[110]*

Herb Gathering

The Root-Cutters, one of the lost plays of Sophocles, referred to the actual practices used by Medea for gathering herbs. Both the fragmentary quotes contain reference to the use of bronze items, appropriate for a priestess of Hekate as her sacred metal. It is also interesting to note that Medea was described as being naked, which is more likely to be poetic license with her being wild-eyed and shrieking, rather than a standard practice:

> *"Medea receives the juice whitely clouded, oozing from the cutting, while she averts her eyes from her hand; she receives the juice in bronze jars ... These bark baskets shield and hide the ends of the roots*

---

109 Medea, Seneca, C1st CE, trans. Miller.
110 Metamorphoses, Ovid, 8CE, trans. Gregory.

that [Medea] cut with bronze sickles while she was naked, shrieking and wild-eyed."[111]

Another lost Sophocles play *The Colchian Women* was said to contain an invocation of Hekate with Circe demonstrating her skill at herbal magic. The bronze sickle referred to by Sophocles may have been a standard herb-gathering tool, certainly in connection with Hekate's spells. It was also referred to in Virgil's *Aeneid* when the description was given of Dido gathering herbs in preparation for her suicide:

> *"Culls hoary simples, found by Phoebe's light,*
> *With brazen sickles reap'd at noon of night;*
> *Then mixes baleful juices in the bowl,"*[112]

Another detailed description of herb-gathering occurred in the *Argonautica*, when Medea gathered the herbs she would use to help Jason overcome his ordeals:

> *"The dark juice of it, like the sap of a mountain-oak, she had gathered in a Caspian shell to make the charm withal, when she had first bathed in seven ever-flowing streams, and had called seven times on Brimo, nurse of youth, night-wandering Brimo, of the underworld, queen among the dead, -- in the gloom of night, clad in dusky garments. And beneath, the dark earth shook and bellowed when the Titanian root was cut."*[113]

It is clear that details of herb gathering would have been well known to the ancient audience, and so the authors would not have needed to go into great detail.

---

111 The Root-Cutters, Sophocles, C5th BCE, trans. M. Dillon.
112 The Aeneid, Virgil, late C1st BCE, trans. J. Dryden.
113 Argonautica, Book 3, Apollonius Rhodius, C3rd BCE, trans. Seaton.

CHAPTER 12

SACRED BRONZE

Bronze was particularly associated with Hekate as her sacred metal and also with the underworld. Numerous references occurred throughout ancient texts in connection with Hekate and bronze. Bronze is an alloy of copper and tin, which sometimes has other metals added to it. Although the Bronze Age was superseded by the Iron Age, bronze is actually harder and more durable than iron (though not steel), which was however more easily available. This durability resulted in bronze being used as the metal of choice for the stylus to inscribe defixiones, as mentioned in the *Greek Magical Papyri.*[114]

Bronze nails were also often used to pierce the lead sheets of defixiones. Bronze was used for amulets, as may be seen with the disk found at the ancient Roman port of Ostia, depicting Hekate on one side and King Solomon on the other.[115]

When describing Tartarus in the underworld, Hesiod observed that *"Round it runs a fence of bronze."*[116] This is clearly a reference to Hekate's power in the underworld, with her metal being used to keep the Titan gods imprisoned.

---

114 PGM XXXVI.187-201.
115 Museo Ostiense E27278A
116 Theogony, Hesiod, C8th BCE, trans. H.G. Evelyn-White.

Bronze sandals were also linked with Hekate as a symbol of her chthonic power, borne by magicians as a symbol of their affiliation to her. For Hekate was *"the goddess of the brazen sandals"*.[117] The term brazen was used for both bronze and brass in the ancient world, so brazen does not automatically mean brass. Bronze sandals were mentioned in the *Greek Magical Papyri* and a second/third century CE Egyptian lead tablet in sequences of Hekate symbols.[118] The Greek Platonic philosopher Heraclides of Pontus, in his lost dialogue (fourth century BCE), was the first person to report the allegorical legend of Empedocles' death by jumping into the volcano Mount Etna, with only a bronze sandal floating out on the lava to show his passing.

Bronze sickles for herb-gathering were mentioned by Sophocles in *The Root-Cutters* and Virgil in *The Aeneid*, as well as bronze jars for collecting the herbs in the former play. The fifth century Roman Neo-Platonist philosopher Macrobius repeated the earlier association of bronze sickles with gathering herbs for Hekate.[119]

A bronze disk or *sors* from the seventh or sixth century BCE used for divination was found at Avernus near Cumae. The identity of the goddess worshipped at Avernus is uncertain, though we may speculate that it was Hekate, particularly with the bronze and divination connections. Another interesting bronze Hekate item is a triangular bronze patera depicting

---

117 On Images, Porphyry, C3rd CE, trans. E.H. Gifford.
118 PGM IV.2334-38, Supplementum Magicum 49, trans R.G. Edmonds III.
119 Saturnalia, V.19.9-11, Macrobius, C5th CE.

three Hekates found at Pergamon in Turkey (c.50-200 CE).[120]

The bronze rhombus mentioned in Theocritus' *Idylls*, although associated with Aphrodite in the text, also emphasised the power of Hekate through its material and the whirring, as seen in the *Chaldean Oracles* later in connection with the iynx.

The bronze triple Hekate amulet found at Ostia in Italy, with King Solomon on the obverse side performing *hygromanteia* (demon summoning) raises an interesting point regarding transmission of ideas and techniques. King Solomon was famous for the brazen vessel containing demons (or genii in the Arabic versions) which was thrown into the sea. This brazen vessel would later occur in a version of the grimoire, the *Goetia* in the seventeenth century as a means of controlling demons, recalling the earlier connections.[121] Considering the interchangeable use of bronze and brass in the ancient world, we must speculate therefore, as to the possible origins of the brazen vessel from Greek magic being incorporated into the Jewish stories. The cross-fertilisation of Greek and Jewish magic is an area which has not yet been fully explored.

---

120 Now located at Staatliche Museum, Berlin.
121 The Goetia of Dr Rudd, Skinner & Rankine, 2007.

CHAPTER 13

IRON NAILS & RINGS

Iron nails were frequently used to pierce defixiones charms, with the literature of the day recommending the best results from nails previously used in a crucifixion. Lucan gave a graphic and gruesome description in *Pharsalia* of how the witch used her teeth to rip and tear the corpse for useful magical ingredients. We may content ourselves with quoting the relevant phrase, *"She purloins the nails that pierced the hands,"*[122] which emphasised the tendency for magicians to use such nails.

Thus in Lucian's *Philopseudes*, the hero was able to deflect Hekate because *"the Arab gave me the ring made of iron from crosses and taught me the spell of many names."*[123] This when activated produced an apotropaic effect which caused Hekate to return to the underworld:

> *"At the sight of her, I stood stock still, and turned the seal of my Arab's ring inwards; whereupon Hecate smote upon the ground with her dragon's foot, and caused a vast chasm to open, wide as the mouth of Hell."*[124]

The use of crucifixion nails in defixiones may have had parallels in, or influenced, Jewish lore, thus we see

---

122 Pharsalia, Lucan, 60 CE, trans. J.D. Duff.
123 Philopseudes, Lucian, C2nd CE, trans. A.M. Harmon.
124 Philopseudes, Lucian, C2nd CE, trans. H.W. & F.G. Fowler.

in a late text from the *Cairo Geniza,* a charm in Hebrew for love, where the person is advised to *"Take a nail from the wood of someone crucified, and make of it a seal."*[125]

The *'Slander spell to Selene'* found in the *Greek Magical Papyri* (PGM IV.2622-2707) contained instructions to make the protective charm on a magnetite heart (*'magnet that is breathing'*). The charm was made with *"engraved on it Hekate lying about the heart, like a little crescent"*[126], and the coercive offering was stamped *"with a completely iron ring, completely tempered, with a Hekate and the name Barzou Pherba."*[127]

The *'Spell to Selene for Any Purpose'* (PGM IV.2785-2890) also used magnetite (lodestone is another name for the same stone) with three-formed Hekate carved on it. Her left face was that of a dog, the middle a maiden wearing horns (i.e. a lunar crescent) and the right face was a goat.

This phenomenon of depictions showing Hekate with animal heads occurred on a number of occasions in charms, making Hekate one of the few major Greek deities who continued to display the animal-headed forms of ancient Egypt. Significantly the other most noticeably animal-headed god from the Greek pantheon was Hermes, who was frequently associated with Hekate, and was also a liminal deity.

---

125 Magic Spells and Formulae: Aramaic Incantations of Late Antiquity, Naveh & Shaked, 1993.
126 PGM IV.2632-33, trans. E.N. O'Neill.
127 PGM IV.2691-94, trans. E.N. O'Neill.

CHAPTER 14

HEKATE & THE ANGELS

David Aune, in his work *Apocalypticism, Prophecy and Magic in Early Christianity* (2006), wrote:

> *"Hekate's popularity during the Hellenistic and Roman periods centred in southwest Asia Minor, where the ideology of her universal sovereignty, particularly as mistress of the Cosmos, would have made her an obvious rival of the Christ of Christianity."*[128]

From the amount of information regarding Hekate that we have found in early Christian writings, it is clear that she was obviously portrayed as one of the threats to the emergence of Christianity. Christian scholars and theologians like Origen (third century CE), Eusebius of Caesarea (early fourth century CE), Arnobius of Sicca (fourth century CE) and St. Augustine of Hippo (fourth-fifth century CE), all wrote of Hekate, and sought to belittle her.

Despite the hostility of such writers, they have provided a body of references which has been largely overlooked, perhaps due to assumption of bias. Nevertheless there are valuable references in their writings which help us gain more of an insight into Hekate's worship and practices. A significant point of commonality between Hekate and Jesus is the

---

128 Apocalypticism, Prophecy and Magic in Early Christianity, Aune, 2006.

association with angels. The word angel comes from the Greek *angelos* meaning *'messenger'*, and may be associated with many deities as spiritual creatures serving the deity. However Hekate was specifically associated with angels, as may be seen from other contemporary sources such as the *Greek Magical Papyri* and the *Chaldean Oracles*.

In the *'Lunar Spell of Claudianus'* in the *Greek Magical Papyri*, angels were specifically requested from Hekate-Selene. She was asked to *"send forth your angel from among those who assist you"*.[129]

Indeed, we cannot ignore the fact that the hierarchy of types of angel serving under Hekate and described in the *Chaldean Oracles*, the *Iynges*, the *Synocheis* and the *Teletarchai*, seem likely to have provided some of the inspiration for Pseudo-Dionysus the Areopagite.

The triad of angel groups of the *Iynges* (*Wrynecks*, after the bird), the *Synocheis* (*Connecters*) and the *Teletarchai* (*Rulers of Initiation*) all had specific roles. The iynges drew the soul closer to the divine and effectively aided in the process of perfection, and their physical tool (the strophalos) was used to bring down divine power, fulfilling the role of heavenly messenger. The synocheis were associated with the promotion of harmony and unification, and the teletarchai had a purificatory role.

Pseudo-Dionysus wrote a number of works in the early sixth century CE including *Celestial Hierarchy* and *Divine Names*. The former work described the nine orders of angels, in three triads of three orders,

---

129 PGM VII.862-918

mirroring some of the theology found in the *Chaldean Oracles*, and laid the basis for the hierarchies used in the Christian orthodoxy and the grimoires.

CHAPTER 15

COINS

Some images of Hekate found on coins emphasised aspects of her nature not seen in the texts. Thus we see a Hekate with characteristics of Cybele, such as a lion-pulled chariot, on the obverse of a head of Elagabalus (who ruled 218-222 CE). Elagabalus was the short-lived Roman Emperor who briefly introduced the worship of a meteorite symbolising the god El-Gabal (Helios) to Rome in preference to the Roman gods.

Other late second century and early third century coins Roman coins (193-211 CE, and 211-212 CE) showed Hekate with a crescent and kalathos (wine-holder) on her head, bearing a torch and patera (offering-plate) and with a dog at her feet. A coin from Pamphylia (part of modern day Turkey) shows Hekate Triformis with the kalathos on her head, and holding torches and serpents (below).

ASPENDOS COIN FROM PAMPHYLIA.

A Phrygian coin c.250 CE showed Hekate bearing two torches and standing on a globe, recalling the perspective of her portrayed in the *Chaldean Oracles*. This image was also seen on engraved gems, sometimes with a lunar crescent on her head.[130]

A Greek coin from the region of Bactria, in what is now northern Afghanistan, shows a fascinating image of Zeus holding a staff in his left hand, and Hekate Triformis bearing two torches in his right hand (below). The image would be very appropriate for the theology of the *Chaldean Oracles*, were it not for the fact that the date of the coin is 185-170 BCE, preceding the *Chaldean Oracles* by several centuries.

GREEK TETRADRACHM COIN FROM BACTRIA.

An early fourth century BCE (c.394-350 BCE) coin showed the head of Hekate on one side and Pegasus on the obverse. This connection may seem obscure, until we consider that Pegasus was said to be fathered by

---

130 E.g. gem 1128, A Catalogue of Engraved Gems in the British Museum, Smith, 1888.

the sea god Poseidon, who was sometimes associated with Hekate. Also the mother of Pegasus was Medusa, the snake-haired Gorgon, who was sometimes considered to be one of the host of beings subservient to Hekate.

Another fourth century BCE coin from Pherae in Thessaly depicts the head of Hekate wearing a laurel wreath on one side, with the Argosian nymph Hypereia on the obverse with her right hand on a lion-head fountain (below). The lion connection is interesting, recalling the link between Hekate and lions.

TRIOBOL COIN FROM THESSALY

Byzantine coins celebrated Hekate through the symbol of the crescent and the star. When Philip of Macedon (father of Alexander the Great) laid siege to the city of Byzantium in 339 BCE, the citizens were saved by Hekate, as they perceived it. Stephen of Byzantium (sixth century CE) in his *Ethnica* related how Philip's troops had dug a concealed entrance and were going to attack by night, but that Hekate being Brilliant (i.e. she was the moon), she caused torches to appear to the citizens, revealing the attack and foiling it. The emblem of the crescent and star which honoured Hekate on the coins was subsequently adopted by the Turks as their design after they captured the city in 1453 CE. Although other legends have replaced this one for the origin of their flag, Hekate was the original goddess behind it![131]

An interesting trend may be seen when looking at the dates of coins depicting and representing Hekate, which is that they were largely from the third or even fourth century CE. This level of popularity shows that Hekate continued to have a strong following which lasted well into the late Roman period at a time when Christianity already had an established foothold in parts of Europe.

---

131 On Ancient Meteorites, and on the Origin of the Crescent and Star Emblem, Antoniadi, 1939

CHAPTER 16

FROM SLEEP

Dreams and nightmares were both attributed to Hekate, who could equally send nightmares to somebody who had offended her as good dreams to someone who propitiated her. This may be seen in PGM LXX, where the charm could be used either to reveal answers to questions during sleep (dream oracle) or to cause somebody else not to sleep. The dream oracle was a function that Hekate shared with her mother, the goddess Asteria.

In a clear example of magical cross-fertilisation, the Jewish *Sepher ha-Razim* (*Book of Mysteries*), which may be dated to the fourth century CE, contained a spell to prevent sleep using the head of a black dog which had never seen the light. The use of a black dog clearly echoed the sacrifice of black dogs to Hekate. Additionally the rubric stated that *"you may bind him with fetters of iron, and restrain him with bars of bronze"*,[132] recalling the sacred metals used in magic associated with Hekate.

Another piece from the *Sepher ha-Razim* called upon Hermes Chthonia by his title of Ram-bearer to bring a ghost for questioning.[133] The offerings made were from a bowl of oil and honey, as in Greek

---

132 Sepher ha-Razim 2.57-72, C4th CE, trans. P.S. Alexander.
133 Sepher ha-Razim 1.176-86, C4th CE.

necromantic practice, and the actions were in groups of three, again showing the parallel to Greek practice for such ceremonies.

That there was a strong degree of such cross-fertilisation is evident when comparing some of the material in texts such as the Jewish *Sepher ha-Razim* and the Greek *Hygromanteia* of around the third century CE, which would both contribute ultimately to the most famous of grimoires, the *Key of Solomon*. Likewise the similarity of the material from both these works to the *Greek Magical Papyri*, which were contemporary, shows that this was a regular occurrence.

A fragment from the fifth century BCE Greek poet Aeschylus, known as the *'father of tragedy'* made reference to Hekate's influence in the realm of dreams. He stated:

> "But either thou art frightened of a spectre beheld in sleep and hast joined the revel-rout of nether Hekate."[134]

This was clearly the popular view of this period, as Hippocrates also wrote in the fifth century BCE:

> "If the patient is attended by fears, terrors, and madnesses in the night, jumps up out of his bed and flees outside, they call these the attacks of Hecate or the onslaughts of ghosts."[135]

A specific reference was made in the *Chaldean Oracles* to the provenance of dreams, when dreams were described as coming from Hekate, who was also referred to as the source of souls:

---

134 Fragment 249, Aeschylus, C5th BCE, trans. W Smyth.
135 On the Sacred Disease, Hippocrates, C5th BCE, trans. D. Ogden.

"There also is a zone of dreams which has as its origin the Source of Souls."[136]

Additionally Hekate's role as source and ruler of the angels and daimones was emphasised when the *Chaldean Oracles* described her sending daimones as ominous dreams:

"The others in the middle, the ones who stand on the midmost winds far from the Divine Fire, these you send to mortals as ominous dreams – a shameful task for Daimones."[137]

Later Eusebius, recording Porphyry's writings, made this point in *Praeparatio Evangelica*, when he said of her, *"As ominous dreams thou dost to mortals send."*[138] When Eusebius quoted Porphyry in describing the procedure for creating a Hekate shrine, we find the line:

*"Then to my image offer many a prayer,
And in thy sleep thou shalt behold me nigh."*[139]

Artemidorus the oneiromancer (*'dream interpreter'*) set up a statue to Hekate Phosphorus amongst his shrines at Thera, one of the Cyclades Islands in the southern Aegean Sea. He also set up a throne with a black stone on to represent the goddess, resembling the worship of baetyls associated with Cybele. This was done around 237 BCE, and may indicate a personal perception of cross-fertilisation with Cybele.

---

136 Chaldean Oracles, C2nd CE, trans. S. Ronan.
137 Chaldean Oracles, C2nd CE, trans. S. Ronan.
138 Praeparatio Evangelica, Eusebius, early C4th CE, trans. Des Places.
139 Praeparatio Evangelica, Eusebius, early C4th CE, trans. Des Places.

CHAPTER 17

ORACLES OF HEKATE

Possibly the earliest recorded oracle of Hekate is that given by Pindar in his second Paean in the fifth century BCE. The oracle essentially told the Abderians they would have victory in battle if they attacked the Thracian tribes, and was proved correct:

> *"It was the first of the month when this befell, and the gracious Hekate, the maid of the ruddy feet, was thereby sending us a message that was longing for fulfilment."*[140]

The association of Hekate with oracles was further made by Aristophanes in his fourth century BCE play, *Lysistrata,* when he wrote, *"Theagenes' wife at any rate is sure to come; she has actually been to consult Hecate."*[141]   Medea, the priestess of Hekate, also gave oracles, emphasising the connection between the goddess and prophecy.[142]

One of the most significant oracles given by Hekate was recorded by Porphyry, and commented on Jesus and Christianity. Porphyry, a Neo-Platonic philosopher of the third century CE who followed the works of Plotinus, also studied the Jewish scriptures and attended lectures by the Christian theologian Origen. The oracle from Hekate was probably in response to his

---

140 Paean 2, Pindar, 462 BCE, trans. G. Sandys.
141 Lysistrata, Aristophanes, 410 BCE, trans. Potter.
142 Pythian Odes 4, Pindar, 462 BCE.

own questions, for he was the author of the most significant intellectual anti-Christian writings of his age, *Against the Christians* and *Prophecy from Oracles*. These two books were burned by Christians for centuries, and the campaign against these works by the early Church was so successful that the only surviving fragments of them occur in other works:

> "And to those who ask why he [Jesus] was condemned to die, the oracle of the goddess [Hekate] replied, 'The body, indeed, is always exposed to torments, but the souls of the pious abide in heaven. And the soul you inquire about has been the fatal cause of error to other souls which were not fated to receive the gifts of the gods, and to have the knowledge of immortal Jove. Such souls are therefore hated by the gods; for they who were fated not to receive the gifts of the gods, and not to know God, were fated to be involved in error by means of him you speak of. He himself, however, was good, and heaven has been opened to him as to other good men. You are not, then, to speak evil of him, but to pity the folly of men: and through him men's danger is imminent.'"[143]

Parts of the *Chaldean Oracles* were clearly spoken by Hekate, and this again emphasised her oracular nature, particularly to the theurgists who called on her, with all things being seen:

> "If you call upon Me often you will perceive everything in lion-form. For then neither does the curved mass of Heaven appear, nor the stars shine. The light of the moon is hidden, and the earth is not firmly secured. But all things are seen by flashes of lightning."[144]

Porphyry's work *Prophecy from Oracles* gives a description of Hekate delivered from the words of the goddess herself:

---

143 Prophecy from Oracles, Porphyry, C3rd CE, trans. J.R. King.
144 Chaldean Oracles, C2nd CE, trans. S. Ronan.

"I come, a virgin of varied forms, wandering through the heavens, bull-faced, three-headed, ruthless, with golden arrows; chaste Phoebe bringing light to mortals, Eileithyia; bearing the three synthemata [sacred signs] of a triple nature. In the Aether I appear in fiery forms and in the air I sit in a silver chariot; Earth reins in my black brood of puppies."[145]

Eusebius was one of the people who quoted from Porphyry, and he made it clear that Hekate was known as an oracle, though his references clearly referred to Hekate as described in the *Chaldean Oracles*, rather than the earlier Hellenic Hekate:

"Ne'er mid the immortal gods an idle threat Or unaccomplish'd doom to seers inspir'd Spake Hecate; but from the almighty mind Of Zeus descends in brightest truth array'd. Lo! by my side walks Wisdom with firm step, Leaning on oracles that ne'er can fail. In bonds secure me: for my power divine Can give a soul to worlds beyond the sky."[146]

---

145 Chaldean Oracles, C2nd CE, trans. Johnston.
146 Praeparatio Evangelica, Eusebius, early C4th CE, trans. Des Places.

CHAPTER 18

OFFERINGS

Like the other Greek gods, Hekate expected offerings when she was invoked. We have discussed Hekate Suppers elsewhere, as well as the sequence offerings were made in, and are focusing here on the other recorded instances of offerings to Hekate to explore their form and content.

The sibyl Deiphobe invoked Hekate first to guide the heroes in Virgil's *Aeneid*:

> *"The priestess pours the wine betwixt their horns;*
> *Then cuts the curling hair; that first oblation burns,*
> *Invoking Hecate hither to repair:*
> *A powerful name in hell and upper air."*[147]

When chthonic gods were invoked a fire was usually made to burn the offerings on, whereas a pit would be dug when dealing with daimones and ghosts. Thus in Seneca's *Medea* we see the fires being built:

> *"Now call on Hecate. Prepare the death-dealing rites;*
> *let altars be erected, and let now their fires resound*
> *within the palace."*[148]

Later in the same play Medea again referred to the fire, and indicated her success by the barking of dogs, which she has taken as an omen of success:

> *"My prayers are heard: thrice has bold Hecate bayed*
> *loud, and has raised the accursèd fire with its baleful*

---

147 Aeneid, Virgil, late C1st BCE, trans. Dryden.
148 Medea, Seneca, C1st CE, trans. Miller.

light. Now all my power is marshalled; hither call my sons that by their hands thou mayst send these costly gifts unto the bride."[149]

When Medea called on Hekate to aid her making the charm to protect Jason, we see much of the same formula used in necromancy, except the absence of a pit makes it clear she was specifically invoking the goddess and not her daimones or ghosts:

> *"She made two mounds: the right to Hecate,*
> *The left to Youth – these were her altars, decked*
> *With the boughs shed gathered from near forests,*
> *And at their sides she dug a little moat.*
> *At one thrust of her knife a black sheep fell*
> *Whose veins were emptied at her altars' trough*
> *And into blood she stirred warm milk and wine."[150]*

When Pausanias described rites which took place, he indicated their chthonic nature by reference to pits:

> *"In Titane there is also a sanctuary of Athena, into which they bring up the image of Koronis [mother of Asklepios] . . . The sanctuary is built upon a hill, at the bottom of which is an Altar of the Winds, and on it the priest sacrifices to the winds one night in every year. He also performs other secret rites [of Hekate] at four pits, taming the fierceness of the blasts [of the winds], and he is said to chant as well the charms of Medea."[151]*

In the first century BCE, the Roman lyric poet Horace wrote of witches summoning Hekate, satirising them and providing one of the enduring images of mad hags, scrabbling at the earth to dig the pit for their necromantic offerings:

> *"They began to dig up the earth with their fingernails and to tear a black lamb to pieces. The blood ran into*

---

149 Medea, Seneca, C1st CE, trans. Miller.
150 Metamorphoses, Ovid, 8 CE, trans. Gregory.
151 Description of Greece, Pausanias, C2nd CE, trans. Frazer.

a ditch, to summon up the souls of the dead and make them answer questions."[152]

By contrast the Roman poet Statius writing a century or so later presented a detailed description of the process of offerings for a chthonian ceremony:

"Tiresias entwined their fearsome horns with garlands of dark flowers –
He did this himself – and then, beside the well-known forest, he first poured,
In a hole dug in the earth, nine lavish offerings of wine and gifts of springtime milk,
Actaean drops of honey, and blood that pleases ghosts.
He poured as much as arid earth would drink, then called for logs.
The mournful priest asked that three mounds be raised for Hecate ...
Around these mounds he scattered cypress branches, signs of mourning."[153]

Writing in the third century CE, the philosopher Porphyry recounted a tale of a holy man in his work *On Abstinence,* which emphasised a move away from animal sacrifice and towards using incense, vegetables and first fruits:

"he diligently sacrificed to them at proper times in every month at the new moon, crowning and adorning the statues of Hermes and Hecate, and the other sacred images which were left to us by our ancestors, and that he also honoured the Gods with frankincense, and sacred wafers and cakes."[154]

This approach prevented the accusations of sacrifice levelled at the worship of the Greek and Roman gods by Christians looking for any excuse to try and claim moral superiority.

---

152 Satires I.8, Horace, C1st BCE, trans. G Luck.
153 On Images, Porphyry, C3rd CE, trans. T. Taylor.
154 On Abstinence, Porphyry, C3rd CE, trans. T. Taylor.

Writing in the fifth century BCE, the Greek writer Sophron of Syracuse produced a play entitled *"The women who say they will expel the goddess [Hekate]"*. The apotropaic nature of the fragments of the play (e.g. dog to be sacrificed) implied a propitiatory rite to appease Hekate, perhaps for breaking a taboo or some other act which displeased her. It read:

> *"Sorceress: Put down the table as it is. Grasp a lump of salt in your hands and laurel behind your ears. Now go over to the hearth and sit down. You, give me the sword: bring the dog here. Where is the pitch? Assistant: Here it is.*
> *Sorceress: Take the little torch and the incense. Come, let me have all the doors open! You watch over there. Put the torch out as it is. Let's have silence, while in these ladies' name I do my sparring. Lady Goddess, your banquet and faultless gifts ..."*[155]

Jason was advised by Medea on how to propitiate Hekate, and it is interesting to note that he had to offer honey, to literally *'sweeten her up'.* The formula was one which drew the goddess in person, and like Orpheus on his quest to bring Eurydice back from the underworld, Jason was advised not to look back lest he spoil the desired effects:

> *"And propitiate only-begotten Hecate, daughter of Perses, pouring from a goblet the hive-stored labour of bees. And then, when thou hast heedfully sought the grace of the goddess, retreat from the pyre; and let neither the sound of feet drive thee to turn back, nor the baying of hounds, lest haply thou shouldst maim all the rites and thyself fail to return duly to thy comrades."*[156]

---

155 The women who say they will expel the goddess [Hekate], Sophron, C5th BCE, trans. M. Dillon.
156 Argonautica, Book 3, Apollonius Rhodius, C3rd BCE, trans. Seaton.

Apart from Hekate Suppers, three types of offerings were left at the crossroads for Hekate, all of which were connected with ritual. These were the *katharmata* (*'offscourings'*), *katharsia* *'(cleansings')* and *oxuthumia* (*'sharp anger'*).

The first of these, the *katharmata*, was the offering of portions of the sacrifice not used in the ceremony such as waste blood and water. In one of the few remaining fragments of his work, the fifth century BCE Athenian poet Eupolis mentioned these offscourings being burned.[157] This term was also sometimes applied to people, specifically those used as scapegoats and sacrificed to deal with natural disasters where the gods needed to be propitiated, such as drought or plague.

The second kind (*katharsia*) was the actual remains of sacrifices, such as eggs and the bodies of dogs. The Roman historian Plutarch mentioned this in *Roman Questions* when he wrote *"dogs are carried out to Hecate with the other katharsia"*[158] and also *"When it [the dog] is sent to crossroads as a supper for the earth-goddess Hecate, it has its due portion among sacrifices that avert and expiate evil."*[159] We know sacrifices to chthonic deities were always black, and that black dogs were sacrificed to her, hence the reference to Hekate in the *Greek Magical Papyri* as a black bitch.

The third kind (*oxuthumia*) was a baked clay censer used to fumigate the house for protection, and then taken and left at the crossroads. It could also describe the rubbish which was taken and burned on the

---

157 Fragment 120, Eupolis, C5th BCE, trans. R. Parker.
158 Roman Questions, Plutarch, late C1st CE, trans. R. Parker.
159 Roman Questions, Plutarch, late C1st CE, trans. R. Parker

censer, as may be seen by the speech given by Electra in Aeschylus' *The Choephori*:

> *"Or shall I pour this draught for Earth to drink,*
> *Sans word or reverence, as my sire was slain,*
> *And homeward pass with unreverted eyes,*
> *Casting the bowl away, as one who flings*
> *The household cleansings to the common road?"*[160]

---

160 The Choephori, Aeschylus, 450 BCE, trans. Anon.

CHAPTER 19

HEKATE SUPPERS

"You see Hecate's faces turned in three directions, To guard the crossroads branching several ways"[161]

A practice particularly associated with the sacred three-way crossroads of Hekate was the Hekate Supper, or *deipna Hekates*. It may be that these offerings were made to appease ghosts and keep them at the crossroads, avoiding trouble from them whilst travelling etc. Alternatively these offerings were described as being made to placate the goddess and ensure that she would look favourably upon those who made regular offerings.

It has been suggested that the crossroads was sacred to Hekate due to her having been abandoned at a crossroads as a baby by her mother Pheraea, and then rescued and brought up by shepherds. This Thessalian tale comes from a scholiast to Lycophron's third century BCE play *Alexandria* (verse 1180), and was a late invention.

Aristophanes recorded that offerings to Hekate were made *"on the eve of the new moon"* – that is when the first sliver of the new moon is visible. There are references to the offerings being made on the thirtieth day of the month, but keep in mind that this was

------

161 Fasti, Ovid, 8 CE, trans. A.S. Kline.

calculated on the Greek calendars, it would vary from state to state as there was no uniformity in the calendar system being used. Our view agrees with K.F. Smith, who in his article *Hekate's Suppers*[162] suggested that it may have been on the first night that the moon was visible again, signifying a possible connection with Hekate as a lunar goddess, rising, like the moon, from the underworld on the night of the new moon.

It has further been suggested that the offerings made at the Hekate Suppers were a form of charity, and certainly the consumption of the food by the poor was noted by the satirist Aristophanes in his fifth century BCE play *Plutus*, as well as by later writers:

> *"Ask Hekate whether it is better to be rich or starving; she will tell you that the rich send her a meal every month and that the poor make it disappear before it is even served."*[163]

The tenth century Byzantine encyclopaedia, the Suda, paraphrased this quote and added a scholion to it:

> *"'From her one may learn whether it is better to be rich or to go hungry. For she says that those who have and who are wealthy should send her a dinner each month, but that the poor among mankind should snatch it before they put it down.' For it was customary for the rich to offer loaves and other things to Hekate each month, and for the poor to take from them."*[164]

Various sources mention different foods offered to Hekate at the suppers. These were:

---

162 Article by K.F. Smith reprinted in The Goddess Hekate Edited by Stephen Ronan.
163 Plutus, Aristophanes, 380 BCE, trans. anon.
164 Suda, Epsilon 363, C10th CE, trans. W. Hutton.

Name	Food	Notes
Magides	A type of loaf or cake	Ingredients and shape unknown
Mainis	Sprat	
Skoroda	Garlic	
Trigle	Mullet	
Psammeta	Sacrificial cake	Described by Harpocration as *"somewhat like the psaista"*
Oon	Eggs	Raw according to a scholiast on Lucian's *Tyrannus* and Clement of Alexandria's *Stromata*
Tyros	Cheese	
Basunias	A type of cake	

Another type of food offering which was left to Hekate on the eve of the full moon, was the *amphiphon,* a type of cake. *Amphiphon* means *light-about,* an appropriate name for this flat cheesecake which was surrounded by small torches.[165]

The supper, or leaving of offerings at the crossroads was one of the hardest practices for the Christian church to stamp out. Records indicate it was still taking place in the eleventh century CE, and it may well have continued far longer in places.

---

165 The Deipnosophists, Athanaeus, C3rd CE.

CHAPTER 20

INVOCATION

Seneca gave a detailed description of the summoning of Hekate, which supplied useful details, reinforcing those found in other writings. Thus we see reference to the state of the conjuror's hair, the use of blood, the fire, and the use of bronze instruments:

> *"You have given forth your voice, ye altars; I see my tripods shaken by the favouring deity. I see Trivia's swift gliding car, not as when, radiant, with full face, she drives the livelong night, but as when, ghastly, with mournful aspect, harried by Thessalian threats, she skirts with nearer rein the edge of heaven. So do thou wanly shed from thy torch a gloomy light through air; terrify the peoples with new dread, and let precious Corinthian bronzes resound, Diktynna, to thy aid. To thee on the altar's bloody turf we perform thy solemn rites; to thee a torch caught up from the midst of a funeral pyre has illumed the night; to thee, tossing my head and with bended neck, I have uttered my magic words; for thee a fillet, lying in funeral fashion, binds my flowing locks; to thee is brandished the gloomy branch from the Stygian stream; to thee with bared breast will I as a maenad smite my arms with the sacrificial knife. Let my blood flow upon the altars; accustom thyself, my hand, to draw the sword and endure the sight of beloved blood."[166]*

A repeated theme illustrating the arrival of the goddess was the behaviour of dogs, barking or

---

166 Medea, Seneca, C1st CE, trans. Miller.

trembling, as seen in examples from writers including
Theocritus and Virgil:

> "And to Hekate Chthonia, before whom even the dogs
> tremble as she moves among the graves and the dark
> blood of the dead."[167]
> "Then, earth began to bellow, trees to dance
> And howling dogs in glimmering light advance
> Ere Hecate came."[168]

Ovid also provided a graphic description of the
invocation of Hekate, emphasising the triple motif used
in the process:

> "Three times she raised her arms to stars and sky,
> And three times wheeled about and three times
> splashed
> Her hair with moonlit water from a brook.
> Three times she screamed,
> then fell upon her knees
> To pray: 'O night, night, night!
> Whose darkness holds
> All mysteries in shade, O flame-lit stars,
> Whose golden rays with Luna floating near
> Are like the fires of day – and you, O Hecate,
> Who know untold desires that work our will
> And art the mistress of our secret spells.'"[169]

Ovid also described the result of a successful
invocation in flowery language:

> "When you have entered me,
> As if a miracle had drained their banks and courses,
> I've driven back rivers to springs and fountains.
> I shake the seas or calm them at my will;
> I whip the clouds or make them rise again;
> At my command winds vanish or return,
> My very spells have torn the throats of serpents,
> Live rocks and oaks are overturned and felled,
> The forests tremble and the mountains split,

---

167 Idylls, Theocritus, 210 BCE, trans. G Luck.
168 The Aeneid, Virgil, late C1st BCE, trans. J. Dryden.
169 Metamorphoses, Ovid, 8 CE, trans. Gregory.

*And deep Earth roars while ghosts walk from their
tombs.*
*Though crashing brass and bronze relieve your
labours,*
Even you, O moon, I charm from angry skies."[170]

To the theurgists of the *Chaldean Oracles*, Hekate's
arrival was something to look forward to, a point she
also made in her own words:

> "*After daybreak, airy, boundless, full of stars, I left
> the great undefiled House of God and descended to
> life-nourishing earth at your request, and by the
> persuasion of ineffable words with which mortal man
> delights in gladdening the hearts of immortals.*"[171]

---

170 Metamorphoses, Ovid, 8 CE, trans. Gregory.
171 Chaldean Oracles, C2nd CE, trans. S. Ronan.

CHAPTER 21

HYMNS

In the context of the ancient world, a hymn was a lyrical religious poem, usually in praise of a deity. There were several hymns to or including Hekate, including the *Orphic Hymn to Hekate*, the *Homeric Hymn to Demeter*, and the *Proclus Hymn to Hekate and Janus*. We have included translations of the *Proclus Hymn to Hekate and Janus*, and the *Prayer to Selene for any operation*, from the *Greek Magical Papyri*, which also takes the form of a hymn and is actually focused on Hekate.

Proclus Hymn to Hekate and Janus

> *Hail, many-named Mother of the Gods,*
> *whose children are fair*
> *Hail, mighty Hekate of the Threshold*
> *And hail to you also Forefather Janus,*
> *Imperishable Zeus*
> *Hail to you Zeus most high.*
> *Shape the course of my life with luminous Light*
> *And make it laden with good things,*
> *Drive sickness and evil from my limbs.*
> *And when my soul rages about worldly things,*
> *Deliver me purified by your soul-stirring rituals.*
> *Yes, give me your hand I pray*
> *And reveal to me the pathways of divine guidance*
> *that I long for,*
> *Then shall I gaze upon that precious Light*
> *Whence I can flee the evil of our dark origin.*
> *Yes, give me your hand I pray,*

And when I am weary bring me to the haven
of piety with your winds.
Hail, many-named Mother of the Gods,
whose children are fair
Hail, mighty Hekate of the Threshold
And hail to you also Forefather Janus,
Imperishable Zeus,
Hail to you Zeus most high.[172]

Initially this juxtaposition of Hekate and Janus might seem curious. However Janus was also a liminal deity specifically associated with the threshold like Hekate. Also in later sources Hekate was suggested as the parent of Janus, thus Arnobius wrote in the fourth century CE:

"Janus, who, they say, being sprung from Coelus and Hecate"[173]

Prayer to Selene for any operation

O three-faced Selene, come to me beloved mistress
Graciously hear my sacred spells:
Image of Night, Youthful One,
Dawn-born light-bringer to mortals
Who rides upon fierce-eyed bulls.
O Queen, you who drive your chariot
On equal course with Helios,
You dance with the triple forms of the triple Graces
As you revel with the stars.
You are Justice and the thread of the Fates,
Clotho, Lachesis and Atropos,
O Three-headed One you are
Persephone, Megaira and Allecto
O One of many shapes who arm your hands
With terrible dark-glowing lamps,

---

172 Hymn to Hekate and Janus, Proclus, C5th CE, trans. S. Ronan.
173 Against the Heathen, Arnobius, C4th CE, trans. Bryce & Campbell.

Who shakes locks of fearsome serpents at your brow,
Whose mouths send forth the roar of bulls,
Whose womb is thick with reptile scales,
At whose shoulders are rows of venomous serpents,
Bound across your back beneath murderous chains.
O Night-bellower, Lover of solitude,
Bull-faced and Bull-headed One
You have the eyes of bulls and the voice of dogs.
Your forms are hidden in the legs of lions.
Your ankle is wolf-shaped,
and savage dogs are friendly to you,
Wherefore they call you Hekate, Many-named, Mene,
Cleaving the air like arrow-shooting Artemis,
O Goddess of Four faces, Four names, Four ways,
Artemis, Persephone, Deer-shooter, Night-shiner,
Thrice-resounding, Triple-voiced, Three-headed, Thrice-named Selene
O Trident-bearing One of Three faces,
Three necks, Three Ways,
Who holds undying flaming fire in triple baskets.
You frequent the Three-ways
and are Mistress of the Three Decads.
Be gracious unto me who is invoking you
and hearken favourably.
You encompass the vast world at night,
You make the Daemones shudder
and the Immortals tremble,
O Many-named Goddess who brings glory to men,
Whose children are fair, O Bull-eyed One, Horned One,
Nature, All-mother, who brings forth both Gods and men,
You roam around Olympus and traverse
the wide and fathomless Abyss,
You are the Beginning and End, and you alone are
Mistress of All:
For from you are All things, and in you,
Eternal One, do All things end.
You bear at your brow an everlasting diadem,
The unbreakable and irremovable bonds of great Cronos,
And you hold in your hands a golden sceptre
Which is encircled by a formula
inscribed by Cronos himself
Who gave it to you to bear in
order that all things remain steadfast:

'Overpowerer and Overpowered One,
Conqueror of men and Damnodamia.'
You rule Chaos, Araracharara ēphthisikēre,
Hail Goddess and attend your epithets.
I offer you this incense Child of Zeus
Arrow-shooter, Heavenly One, Goddess of Harbours,
Mountain-roamer, Goddess of Crossroads,
Nocturnal One of the Underworld, Shadowy One of Hades,
Still One who frightens, having a feast among the graves.
You are Night, Darkness and broad Chaos,
For you are Necessity hard to escape
You are Fate, you are Erinys and the Torture,
You are the Murderess and Justice
You hold Cerberus in chains,
You are steely-blue with serpent-scales,
O serpent-haired and Serpent-girdled One,
Blood-drinker, Death-bringer who breeds corruption,
Feaster on hearts,
Flesh-eater who devours those who died before their time,
Grave-resounder,
Driver to the Wanderings of Madness,
Come to my sacrifices and fulfil this task for me.[174]

The offering for positive magic was storax, myrrh, sage, frankincense, and a fruit pit. For malevolent magic, the offering was more animal-based, being the magical material of a dog and a dappled goat (or in a similar way, of a virgin untimely dead).

The protective charm for the rite used a lodestone with a three-faced Hekate carved on it. The faces were of a dog (left), a maiden wearing horns (middle), and a goat (right). It was cleaned with natron[175] and water, and dipped in the blood of a person who died a violent

---

174 PGM IV.2785-2870, pre C4th CE, trans. S. Ronan.

175 A salt used by the Egyptians in embalming and purification.

death. A food offering was made to the charm and the previous spell rubric repeated.

Although this hymn was addressed to Selene, it was clearly a hymn to Hekate. The confusion of title probably arose from the syncretisation of the goddesses in the hymn, with Selene being mentioned first. As well as Selene, other goddesses including Artemis, Persephone, and Mene were mentioned. The reference to the Three Fates may be drawn from Porphyry's third century work *On Images*, where he wrote of Hekate:

> *"And, again, the Fates are referred to her powers, Clotho to the generative, and Lachesis to the nutritive, and Atropos to the inexorable will of the deity."*[176]

There was also a short example of voces magicae. The choice of offerings for doing good or harm emphasised the versatility of the uses of the hymn. In keeping with other contemporary magical practices, fragrant resins and herbs were used for beneficent magic, with bones or body parts (the 'magical material') being used for malefic magic.

---

176 On Images, Porphyry, C3rd CE, trans. T. Taylor.

CHAPTER 22

ANIMAL FORMED

Of all the Greek gods, none are portrayed with animal heads as often as Hekate, demonstrating her connection to the more primal forces of the past. Through considering the animals associated with Hekate we gain further insights into her powers, and how they crossed every boundary.

When she was described three-formed with three heads, Hekate was seen with different combinations of animal heads. These included the cow, dog, dragon, goat, horse, and serpent. There were also references in later texts to Hekate being four-headed, in the *Greek Magical Papyri* and *Liber De Mensibus*.

Cow-Headed/Bull-Headed

Pitys spell of attraction in the *Greek Magical Papyri* included a three-formed Hekate drawn on a flax leaf with cow, maiden and dog heads.[177] In this category we must also include the image of bull-headed Hekate. In the *Prayer to Selene for any spell*[178] she was described as *"O Night-bellower, Lover of solitude, Bull-faced and Bull-headed One"* and *"bull-eyed, horned, mother of gods and men."*

---

177 PGM IV.2006-2125.
178 PGM IV.2785-2870, pre C4th CE, trans. S. Ronan.

John Lydus in his work *Liber De Mensibus* described Hekate as being four-headed, with one of these heads being *"the head of a bull, which snorts like some bellowing spirit, is raised towards the sphere of air"*[179]

ANIMAL HEADED HEKATE, FROM CARTARI, 1571

179 De Mensibus, Lydus, C6th CE, trans. Wunsch.

Dog-Headed

The *Prayer to Selene for any spell* in the *Greek Magical Papyri* included a charm made from lodestone with a three-formed Hekate with dog, horned maiden and goat heads[180] and *Pitys spell of attraction* also included a three-formed Hekate with dog head.

John Lydus *Liber De Mensibus* described one of her four heads being *"that of a dog as having a punishing and avenging nature is raised towards the sphere of earth."*[181]

Dragon-Headed

The tenth century Byzantine encyclopaedia the *Suda* paraphrased Pseudo-Nonnos' *Commentaries on the Orations of Gregory Nazianzenus*, describing Hekate thus:

> *"Some [say that she is] Artemis, others the moon, appearing in strange manifestations for those invoking curses. Her manifestations [are] humans with the heads of dragons, and of immense size, so that the sight stupefies those who see it."* [182]

This late description united the dragon imagery associated with Medea as the steeds pulling her chariot in some of the tales with the immense size associated with Hekate in stories like Lucian's *Philopseudes*, where she was also described as having dragon's feet.

---

180 PGM IV.2785-2890.
181 De Mensibus, Lydus, C6th CE, trans. Wunsch.
182 Suda Epsilon 364, C10th CE, trans. W. Hutton.

MEDEA AND THE DRAGON CHARIOT, BY SOLIS 1581

Goat-Headed

The Prayer to Selene lodestone charm depicted a three-formed Hekate with dog, horned maiden and goat heads.[183] The goat was one of the animals named in the list of Hekate symbols in the prayer given in the *Greek Magical Papyri* (PGM VII.756-94).

Horse-Headed

The *Chaldean Oracles* gave a description of forms in which Hekate could appear when called, and this included, *"a horse flashing more brightly than light."*[184]

There are also references in the *Greek Magical Papyri* to Hekate in connection with horses. One spell asked for the opponent to be restrained in a horse

---

183 PGM IV.2785-2890.
184 Chaldean Oracles, C2nd CE, trans. S. Ronan.

race,[185] a theme which was seen in the defixiones curse tablets as well. In the *Spell of Attraction*[186], Hekate was described as *"horse-faced goddess"*. The horse was also one of the animals named in the list of Hekate symbols in the prayer given in the *Greek Magical Papyri* (PGM VII.756-94).

John Lydus *Liber De Mensibus* described one of her four heads being *"the fire-breathing head of a horse is clearly raised towards the sphere of fire"*[187]

A marble frieze from Crannon in Thessaly from the fourth century BCE shows Hekate with a dog beside her placing a wreath on a mare's head. As this was dedicated by a race-horse owner it may well be that this was simply a personal devotion or petition. Nevertheless it does provide another image linking Hekate with horses.

Serpent-Headed

A number of the descriptions of Hekate described her as having serpents coiled around her, and serpents for hair or in her hair. Whilst this is not strictly snake-headed, we felt it appropriate to mention these images in this section.

In the *Prayer to Selene for any spell*[188] there was a range of serpent imagery associated with Hekate, including, *"You are steely-blue with serpent-scales, O serpent-haired and Serpent-girdled One."* The serpent

---

185 PGM III.1-164.
186 PGM IV.2441-2621.
187 De Mensibus, Lydus, C6th CE, trans. Wunsch.
188 PGM IV.2785-2870, pre C4th CE, trans. S. Ronan.

was one of the animals named in the list of Hekate symbols in the prayer given in the PGM VII.756-94.

The *Chaldean Oracles* included a serpentine reference to Hekate, which said of her, *"the She-Serpent, and the snake-girdled; others calling her on account of her appearance Girt in serpent coils."*[189]

As the hydra was a multiple snake-headed being, we should also mention John Lydus *Liber De Mensibus,* which described one of her four heads being, *"the head of a hydra as being of a sharp and unstable nature is raised towards the sphere of water."*[190]

---

189 Chaldean Oracles, C2nd CE, trans. S. Ronan.
190 De Mensibus, Lydus, C6th CE, trans. Wunsch.

CHAPTER 23

NECROMANCY & REANIMATION

Necromancy deals with communication between the living and the dead, and crosses the liminal barrier of death. As such it is a form of magic which has been specifically associated with Hekate and other underworld deities. Hekate as the queen of the restless dead was particularly appropriate to call upon, as the restless dead were the type most often called upon for assistance in magic. In this the Greeks continued the Egyptian tradition of calling on the dead for assistance with spells due to their greater level of personal magical power.

The restless dead were those who did not receive proper burial rites, or who died violently or before their time. These factors were often combined, with many soldiers killed in battle not receiving proper burials, and this resulted in battlegrounds being a favoured place to perform necromancy. In his work *Pharsalia*, Lucan described his witch Erictho being keen that battles should take place in Thessaly to give her an ample supply of body parts for magic and sites for performing necromancy.

The first account of necromancy in Greek myths was given about Circe, the priestess (or some say daughter) of Hekate, in Homer's *Odyssey*. Circe explained to Odysseus what he needed to do to successfully perform his necromancy, and this template set the scene for future literary descriptions of necromancy:

> *"'When you have reached this spot, as I now tell you, dig a trench a cubit or so in length, breadth, and depth, and pour into it as a drink-offering to all the dead, first, honey mixed with milk, then wine, and in the third place water - sprinkling white barley meal over the whole. Moreover you must offer many prayers to the poor feeble ghosts, and promise them that when you get back to Ithaca you will sacrifice a barren heifer to them, the best you have, and will load the pyre with good things. More particularly you must promise that Teiresias shall have a black sheep all to himself, the finest in all your flocks."[191]*

Although in the modern world necromancy is shunned, communication with the dead remains an established part of western culture, as can be seen by the popularity of mediums and the Spiritualist church. Bodies are not involved in these practices, but they are still a continuation of the process of questioning the dead for answers or comfort.

In the ancient Greek world, the standard procedure for necromancy was the same as the offerings made to the dead for funerals:

- Dig a pit
- Make a fire
- Make libations of liquids such as honey and milk, oil, water, wine
- Offer grain (including barley cakes) and flowers
- Sacrifice (black) animal and burn on fire
- Offer blood
- Prayers to Chthonic gods

---

191 Odyssey, Homer, B8th BCE, trans. S. Butler

This suggests that the key difference between a funeral to bury the dead and an act of necromancy to communicate with the dead was the intent. The similarity was emphasised in texts like Seneca's *Medea*, describing the practitioner's hair being unbound or loosely tied for necromancy, as was the case for funerals. Offerings to the gods were burned on the fire, whereas offerings to the ghosts of the dead were made into the pit, literally into the earth.

In his writings Horace introduced a new element into necromantic ritual, with the use of wax dolls as vessels for the summoned spirits by his witches Canidia and Sagana. This was the first literary reference to the use of such figures, which have subsequently been used in a variety of traditions like Voodoo, Wicca and Witchcraft, and are known as voodoo dolls, poppets or fith-faths. This has also resulted in Erictho being described as the *"first recognizably modern witch in European literature."*[192]

> *"They had two dolls – one of wax, the other, larger one of wool; [the wool one] was meant to punish the smaller, waxen one, which stood submissive like a slave about to be put to death. One of the witches called 'Hecate!,' the other 'Dreadful Tisiphone!" You could see serpents sliding, hell hounds running. The moon blushed because she refused to be witness to all this and hid behind some large monuments."*[193]

In Euripides' *Helen* the two contrasting sides of Hekate were portrayed, with Menelaus emphasising Hekate Phosphorus as the light-bringer, whereas Helen by contrast emphasised Hekate Chthonia the ruler of ghosts and daimones:

---

192 Momentary Monsters: Lucan and His Heroes, W.R. Johnson, 1987.
193 Satires I.8, Horace, 35 BCE, trans. C. Faraone.

"Menelaus: O Hecate, giver of light, send thy visions favourably!
Helen: In me thou beholdest no spectre of the night, attendant on the queen of phantoms."[194]

Reanimation is a form of necromancy, and this was described in the tales of Medea and Lucan's Erictho, both in a manner which resembles a full blood transfusion, though initially fatal due to the jugulation and blood draining of the individual being reanimated. Medea jugulated Aeson, drained his blood and prepared fresh blood for him by cooking it up with a range of magical ingredients in her cauldron. Erictho followed a similar procedure, and both witches' mixtures included a range of animal parts and herbs. Medea was described as using Thessalian roots emphasising the connection between dubious magic and foreign realms.

MEDEA JUGULATING AESON BY BAUR, 1659

The poet Shelley was a keen fan of Lucan, and read the Roman poet's works to his wife Mary. The

---

194 Helen, Euripides, 412 BCE, trans. E.P. Coleridge.

description by Lucan of the witch Erictho collecting body parts and reanimating bodies is now commonly thought of as providing the inspiration for her classic novel *Frankenstein*.

As well as literary figures, the magician Empedocles also claimed to be able to reanimate the dead, telling students, *"and you will fetch back from Hades the life-force of a man who has died."*[195] The rest of this fragment referred to control of the weather and the rejuvenating of old age, both powers particularly associated with Medea and other followers of Hekate in the literature of ancient Greece.

Many writers in the ancient world emphasised the foreign nature of such magicians, suggesting that only they would turn to such forms of magic as necromancy or reanimation. Thus the land of Thessaly became the notorious home of witches, Persia, Egypt and Babylon the homes of necromancers. However it is clear that both necromancy and reanimation were part of the practices of the witch or sorceror of the ancient world, as can be seen from the tales of Medea and Erictho through to Lucian in his second century work *Philopseudes*:

> *"he wore brogues, as the Hyperboreans usually do. I need not detain you with the everyday manifestations of his power: how he would make people fall in love, call up spirits, resuscitate corpses, bring down the Moon, and show you Hecate herself, as large as life. But I will just tell you of a thing I saw him do at Glaucias's ... Well, as soon as the moon was full, that being the time usually chosen for these enchantments, he dug a trench in the courtyard of the house, and commenced operations, at about midnight,*

---

195 Fragment 111, Empedocles, C5th BCE, trans. P. Kingsley.

by summoning Glaucias's father, who had now been dead for seven months. The old man did not approve of his son's passion, and was very angry at first; however, he was prevailed on to give his consent. Hecate was next ordered to appear, with Cerberus in her train, and the Moon was brought down, and went through a variety of transformations"[196]

The connection between Hekate and necromancy continued for many centuries after the fall of Rome, as witnessed by the references in Shakespeare and other Renaissance writers. Interestingly, and appropriately, Hekate was invoked as part of a necromantic ritual to summon a suicide given by Ebenezer Sibly, in his book *A New and Complete Illustration of the Occult Sciences*, Book 4 (1795):

"But if it be desired to put interrogatories to the spirit of any corpse that hath hanged, drowned, or otherwise made away with itself, the conjuration must be performed while the body hangs, or on the spot where it is first found after the suicide hath been committed, and before it is touched or removed by the coroner's jury. The ceremony is as follows: the Exorcist binds upon the top of his wand a bundle of St. John's wort, or milliès perforatum, with the head of an owl; and, having repaired to the spot where the corpse lies, at twelve o'clock at night, he draws the circle, and solemnly repeats the following words:
By the mysteries of the deep, by the flames of Banal, by the power of the east, and the silence of the night, by the holy rites of Hecate, I conjure and exorcise thee, thou distressed spirit, to present thyself here, and reveal unto me the cause of thy calamity, why thou didst offer violence to thy own liege life, where thou art now in being, and where thou wilt hereafter be."[197]

---

196 Philopseudes, Lucian, C2nd CE, trans. H.W. & F.G. Fowler.
197 A New and Complete Illustration of the Occult Sciences, Sibly, 1795.

CHAPTER 24

DEATH MAGIC

As most of Hekate's magic dealt with liminal events and places, it is unsurprising that she should have been called on at times to produce death, be it of another person or the caller. In this context we may see her as Hekate *Prytania* ('*invincible queen*').

In the *Argonautica*, a description was recorded of how Medea used her magic to kill Talos, the giant brazen man. Inevitably she would have called on Hekate to release the Keres, and it is interesting to note again the triple motif used in the summoning:

> "*She covered both her cheeks with a fold of her purple mantle, and Jason led her by the hand as she passed across the benches. Then, with incantations, she invoked the Keres [Spirits of Death], the swift hounds of Hades who feed on souls and haunt the lower air to pounce on living men. She sank to her knees and called upon them, three times in song, three times with spoken prayers. She steeled herself of their malignity and bewitched the eyes of Talos with the evil in her own. She flung at him the full force of her malevolence, and in an ecstasy of rage she plied him with images of death ... it was thus that Talos, for all his brazen frame, was brought down by the force of Medea's magic. He was hoisting up some heavy stones with which to keep them from anchorage, when he grazed his ankle on a sharp rock and the ichors ran out of him like molten lead. He stood there for a short time, high on the jutting cliff. But even his strong legs could not support him long; he began to*

sway, all power went out of him, and he came down with a resounding crash."[198]

The description given by Virgil in the *Aeneid* of Queen Dido preparing for her suicide after being rejected by Aeneas, supplied more interesting details:

> *"Sad cypress, vervain, yew, compose the wreath,*
> *And ev'ry baleful green denoting death.*
> *The queen, determin'd to the fatal deed,*
> *The spoils and sword he left, in order spread,*
> *And the man's image on the nuptial bed.*
> *And now (the sacred altars plac'd around)*
> *The priestess enters, with her hair unbound,*
> *And thrice invokes the pow'rs below the ground.*
> *Night, Erebus, and Chaos she proclaims,*
> *And threefold Hecate, with her hundred names,*
> *And three Dianas: next, she sprinkles round*
> *With feign'd Avernian drops the hallow'd ground;*
> *Culls hoary simples, found by Phoebe's light,*
> *With brazen sickles reap'd at noon of night;*
> *Then mixes baleful juices in the bowl,*
> *And cuts the forehead of a newborn foal,*
> *Robbing the mother's love. The destin'd queen*
> *Observes, assisting at the rites obscene;*
> *A leaven'd cake in her devoted hands*
> *She holds, and next the highest altar stands:*
> *One tender foot was shod, her other bare;*
> *Girt was her gather'd gown, and loose her hair.*
> *Thus dress'd, she summon'd, with her dying breath,*
> *The heav'ns and planets conscious of her death,*
> *And ev'ry pow'r, if any rules above,*
> *Who minds, or who revenges, injur'd love."[199]*

By committing suicide Dido made herself one of the restless dead, who were associated with curses. There was a Greek belief that the intent at the moment of death was empowered, so Dido was empowering her curse on Aeneas through her action.

---

198 Argonautica, Book 4, Apollonius Rhodius, C3rd BCE, trans. Seaton.
199 The Aeneid, Virgil, late C1st BCE, trans. J. Dryden.

CHAPTER 25

UNDERWORLD

Hekate was frequently called *Chthonia* (*subterranean* or *earthly one*), a title she shared with Demeter, Hermes and Nyx. The term was particularly applied to deities in a chthonic or infernal context, i.e. when they were being associated with the underworld. Chthonic deities were worshipped with altars on the ground, whereas Olympian deities had altars set on objects so they would be in the air (i.e. towards Olympus).

Additionally she was sometimes referred to as *Nexichthon* ('*she who breaks open the earth*'), a title used in the *Greek Magical Papyri*[200] and in a series of Cypriot *defixiones*, where she was called *"you who possess the keys of Hades, who break open the surface of earth"*.[201]

Hekate's title of *Kleidouchos* ('*key-bearer*') was one of those most intimately connected to her underworld roles, for she bore the keys to the underworld, and determined who went to the paradisiacal part known as the Elysian Fields. In this context she oversaw the appropriate location of the soul of the deceased at the end of its journey.

---

200 PGM IV.2722.
201 Defixionum Tabellae, Audollent, 1967

Cerberus (or Kerberus) was the ancient Greek triple-headed dog which guarded the entrance to the underworld to prevent any of the spirits of the dead escaping back to the land of the living. Cerberus could be friendly or hostile to new arrivals entering Hades, though if they brought him honey cakes he was more likely to be friendly. He was first mentioned without reference to his name as the dog of Hades in the *Iliad* and the *Odyssey*.

Hesiod in his *Theogony* described Cerberus by name, and gave his parentage as the immortals Typhon and Echidna. He was described as being brazen-voiced and fifty-headed. It was the Greek scholar Apollodorus in the second century BCE who gave the now familiar description of Cerberus as a three-headed dog with a dragon's tail and a back covered with snakes. A number of images on vases show Cerberus with two heads, and in one instance he was described as having one hundred heads.

HERCULES DRAGING CERBERUS FROM THE UNDERWORLD, KRAUSS 1670

Cerberus was dragged into the daylight by the semi-divine Hercules as the last of his twelve labours, with the assistance of the goddess Persephone. The saliva from Cerberus' jaws formed the poisonous psychoactive herb aconite when it touched the earth. It has been suggested that his name Cerberus comes from Ker Erebus, or *demon of darkness*. Certainly this would explain why the philosopher Porphyry declared that Cerberus was one of the chief daimones. Agrippa quoted Porphyry as saying that Cerberus was *"conversant in three elements, Air, Water and Earth, a most pernicious devil."*[202] However this contradicts Porphyry's remark in *On Images*, when he wrote:

> *"Cerberus is represented with three heads, because the positions of the sun above the earth are three - rising, midday, and setting."*[203]

The *Greek Magical Papyri* contained an attraction spell to draw a potential lover which called upon Cerberus. This required the person to make a wax figure of a dog eight fingers long, and place a bone from the head of a man who had died violently in its mouth. Characters were inscribed on the sides of the dog and it was placed on a tripod, and its right paw raised. Beneath the dog on the tripod was placed a strip of papyrus with the words *Iao Asto Iophe* and the name of the desired person. After speaking the words of the spell, if the dog hissed the person was not coming, and if it barked they were.

The spell adjured Cerberus by the restless dead, specifically suicides by hanging and those who had died violently, and contained a list of *voces magicae*. The recipient was named twice, as was her mother, to ensure the correct person was targeted.[204]

---

202 Of Occult Philosophy, Book 3, Agrippa, 1533.
203 On Images, Porphyry, C3rd CE, trans. E.H. Gifford.
204 PGM IV.1872-1927.

CHAPTER 26

BLACK DOGS

Hekate's association with dogs was pre-eminent, with dogs being her companions, her heralds and her offerings. We know that black dogs were sacrificed to Hekate at the crossroads as her cult animal, including black puppies. The sacrifice of dogs to Hekate is one of the indicators used today to suggest that she was not originally a Greek goddess, as dog sacrifices were associated with a small number of gods, all of whom were foreign.

Many authors referred to dogs barking to announce her presence, a useful sign for those calling for her aid:

> *"A baying of hounds was heard through the half-light: the goddess was coming, Hecate."*[205]

The dog as the companion to Hekate was said to derive from the tale of queen Hekabe (note the similarity in name). After the city of Troy fell, queen Hekabe, the wife of king Priam, went with Odysseus as his captive. On the voyage back to Greece Hekabe saw her son Polydor's' corpse on a beach, murdered by the Thracian king Polymestor, who had been looking after him with a healthy sized treasure he coveted. Incensed, Hekabe killed the king and was attacked and stoned by the locals, but the gods transformed her into

---

205 Aeneid, Virgil, late C1st BCE, trans. J. Dryden.

a black dog, and she became the companion of Hekate. The Thracians used to offer black dogs in sacrifice to the goddess Bendis, who was assimilated into Hekate, so this myth may also represent that assimilation:

> "The maiden daughter of Perseus, Brimo Trimorphos, shall make thee [Queen Hekabe] her attendant, terrifying with thy baying in the night all mortals who worship not with torches the images of Zerynthia [Hekate] queen of Strymon [in Thrace], appeasing the goddess of Pherai with sacrifice. And the island spur of Pakhynos shall hold thine awful cenotaph, piled by the hands of thy master [Odysseus], prompted by dreams when thou hast gotten the rites of death in front of the streams of Heloros. He shall pour on the shore offerings for thee, unhappy one, fearing the anger of the three-necked goddess, for that he shall hurl the first stone at thy stoning and begin the dark sacrifice to Hades."[206]

An image from the Pergamon Frieze (second century BCE) showed Hekate and Artemis battling giants. Hekate is seen in her triple form and her (or Artemis') dog bites the thigh of the giant she is attacking.

Plutarch made the connection between Hekate and the Roman birth goddess, Genetyllis, in the second century CE, through the dog sacrifice and similarity of role:

> "Accordingly, just as the Greeks sacrifice a bitch to Hecate, even so do the Romans offer the same sacrifice to Geneta on behalf of the members of their household."[207]

---

206 Alexandra, Lycophron, C3rd BCE, trans. Mair
207 Roman Questions, Plutarch, C2nd CE, trans. F.C. Babbitt

Several centuries later the sixth century CE Greek chronicler Hesychius of Miletius also recorded that Genetyllis, was associated with Hekate, a link he also emphasised by the dog sacrifice made to Genetyllis for an easy child-birth.

CHAPTER 27

SERPENTS

Serpents were frequently associated with Hekate, being twined about her or close to her. Sophocles described her, saying:

> *"She who is crowned with oak-leaves*
> *And the coils of wild serpents."*[208]

When Hekate appeared to Jason, she was described that *"round her horrible serpents twined themselves among the oak boughs."*[209]

The effects were even more impressive in Ovid's description, for in his words:

> *"a groan came from the ground, the bushes blanched, the spattered sward was soaked with gouts of blood, stones brayed and bellowed, dogs began to bark, black snakes swarmed on the soil and ghostly shapes of silent spirits floated through the air."*[210]

A defixio from first century CE Athens showed a three-formed Hekate, with six arms, bearing torches in the upper pair of arms, with the lower pair being serpentine.[211] Some images of Hekate from Rome also showed her three-formed, holding two torches, knives and whips. This image was used on coins and engraved gems, which also showed two serpents coiled, one on either side of her. Earlier Greek coins show

---

208 The Root-Cutters, Sophocles, C5th BCE, trans. Z. Yardley.
209 Argonautica, Book 3, Apollonius, C3rd CE, trans. R.C. Seaton.
210 Metamorphoses, Ovid, 8 CE, trans. Gregory.
211 Athenian Defixio, first century CE.

Hekate holding a serpent as well as a key, a dagger and torches.[212]

The serpent which guarded the Golden Fleece was also associated with Hekate, dwelling in the middle of her sacred garden. The *Orphic Argonautica* described the snake thus:

> *"A terrible snake, a monster deadly to mortals, which cannot be described. For it was decked with golden scales and it wound up around the trunk in its huge coils ... Untiring but without sleep, it scrutinized its surroundings with grey eyes."*[213]

There was also serpent imagery associated with Hekate in the *Chaldean Oracles*. Thus we see that she was described as *"the snake-girdled the three-headed,"*[214] and *"the She-serpent, and the snake-girdled: others calling her on account of her appearance girt in serpent coils."*[215]

---

212 A Catalogue of the Greek Coins in the British Museum, Head, 1906.
213 Orphic Argonautica, C4th CE, trans. D. Ogden.
214 Chaldean Oracles, C2nd CE, trans. S. Ronan.
215 Chaldean Oracles, C2nd CE, trans. S. Ronan.

CHAPTER 28

THE STROPHALOS

An interesting fragment in the *Chaldean Oracles* reads *"Work with the strophalos of Hekate."*[216] The *strophalos* or *iynx* has been the subject of much debate. The word *iynx* (plural: *iynges*) is the Greek name for the wryneck, a member of the woodpecker family which eats ants. This has created confusion, as a form of magic was performed with a bird tied to a wooden wheel, which was called an iynx wheel. In Pindar's *Pythian Odes*, Aphrodite was described as giving the iynx bird and wheel to Jason to win Medea's love, introducing this form of magic to humanity:

> *"The Queen of sharpest arrows, brought the dappled iynx from Olympus, bound to the four spokes of the indissoluble wheel;"*[217]

The references to its use in love magic for attracting partners clearly seem to refer to this type of iynx. Thus we see a reference in Xenophon's writings to its use, when he had a female courtesan tell Socrates:

> *"I assure you these things don't happen without the help of many potions and spells and magic wheels."*[218]

---

216 Chaldean Oracles, C2nd CE, trans. S. Ronan.
217 Pythian Odes 4.213-15, Pindar, 462 BCE, trans. C. Faraone.
218 Memorabilia, 3.XI.17, Xenophon, C4th BCE, trans. E.C. Marchant & O.J. Todd.

The repeated chorus in Theocritus *Idylls* which declared, *"Draw my lover here, iynx (magic wheel)"*[219] referred to the iynx. In the same text, there is also reference to a bronze rhombus whirling,[220] which hinted at the later type of iynx associated with Hekate and also known as a strophalos.

Moving forward in time, the iynges were also a group of angelic beings named in the *Chaldean Oracles*. It has been suggested that the strophalos bears the name of iynx to indicate its function as a physical symbol of the angelic beings. This idea is supported by a reference in the Greek sophist Philostratus' work *The Life of Apollonius of Tyana*, where in a description of the King of Babylon's judgement chamber, the iynges were called *'the tongues of the gods'*:

> *"And it is here that the king gives judgement, and golden iynges are hung from the ceiling, four in number, to remind him of Adrastea, the goddess of justice, and to engage him not to exalt himself above humanity. These figures the Magi themselves say they arranged; for they have access to the palace, and they call them the tongues of the gods.* "[221]

The main description of the strophalos was given centuries after the *Chaldean Oracles*, by the Byzantine historian and philosopher Michael Psellus in the eleventh century. He wrote:

> *"The strophalos of Hekate is a golden sphere with lapis lazuli enclosed in its centre, which is spun by means of a leather thong, and which is covered with symbols: as it was spun they [the Theurgists] made*

---

219 Idylls 2, Theocritus, 270 BCE, trans. Z. Yardley.
220 Idylls 2, Theocritus, 270 BCE, trans. Z. Yardley.
221 The Life of Apollonius of Tyana, Philostratus the Athenian, early C3rd CE, trans. F.C. Conybeare.

their invocations. These spheres were generally called iynges and could be either spherical or triangular or of some other form. And while they were making their invocations they emitted inarticulate or animal cries, laughing and whipping the air. So the Oracle teaches that it is the motion of the strophalos which works the ritual, on account of its ineffable power. It is called 'of Hekate' as consecrated to Hekate."[222]

Two references in the writings of the last of the Neo-Platonist philosophers, Damascius also implied the role of the iynx as an instrument for directing divine power:

"The Great Hekate emits a life-generating whir."[223]
"The life-generating Goddess ... possesses the separated and manifest whirring-forth of the life-generating light."[224]

Two centuries earlier Eusebius of Caesarea mentioned the iynges in his *Praeparatio Evangelica*, being used as part of the process of conjuration:

"Easily dragging some of these unwilling [divinities] from the Aether by means of ineffable iynges, you lead them earthwards."[225]

The same text included the words of an impatient Hekate who was clearly not impressed with being summoned in such a manner:

"Why do you call me, the goddess Hekate, here from the swift Aether by means of god-compelling necessity."[226]

---

222 Psellus commentary on the Chaldean Oracles, C11th CE, trans. D.J. O'Meara.
223 Difficulties and Solutions of First Principles, Damascius, C6th CE, trans. C.E. Ruelle.
224 Difficulties and Solutions of First Principles, Damascius, C6th CE, trans. C.E. Ruelle.
225 Praeparatio Evangelica, Eusebius, early C4th CE, trans. Des Places.

This emphasised the ability of the magician who followed the correct procedures to compel the attention of the gods, a point that was snatched upon by Christian writers to demonstrate the superiority of their inaccessible God. It has also become a point conveniently ignored by modern writers and practitioners, as being part of the archaic past, and like animal sacrifice, not appropriate to a modern relationship with the ancient gods.

However, the coercive spells and techniques found in the *Greek Magical Papyri* and other contemporary sources were simply continuing a tradition from ancient Egypt. This continued through into the Renaissance grimoires, with the magicians compelling the attention of demons or other spiritual creatures, and has even survived in a diluted form into the Wiccan tradition.

Marinus, the pupil and biographer of the Greek Neo-Platonist philosopher Proclus, wrote in the fifth century CE that the iynges were used to bring rain when Attica was suffering from a drought, again drawing heavenly influence down to earth.[227]

---

226 Praeparatio Evangelica, Eusebius, early C4th CE, trans. Des Places.
227 Life of Proclus, Marinus, C5th CE.

CHAPTER 29

KING SOLOMON

Considering the level of cross-fertilisation between Hellenic and Jewish spirituality, the extent to which Greek magic was conflated with Jewish magic is another point we need to explore. The connection between Hekate and Jewish magic is found both in the *Greek Magical Papyri* and on amulets. The *Love Spell of Attraction* (PGM XXXVI.187-201) contained the Hebrew names Adonai (*'Lord'*), and Sabaoth ([*God of*] *'Hosts'*), and IAO. Adonai was the major divine name, used initially as a substitute and then as a replacement for IHVH, the Tetragrammaton or Unpronounceable Name of God.

IAO was a Gnostic contraction of IHVH, which was also connected to Hekate through the defixiones, as when it was combined with the name Brimo to form a composite name, Brimiao. The same text also included long strings of *voces magicae*, including the name Adonai:

> *"I invoke you by the unconquerable god, Iao Barbathiao Brimiao Chermari."*[228]

This particular defixio from fifth century CE Upper Egypt was unique in that it was wrapped around two wax figurines in an embrace and sealed in a pot. This use of wax figurines would subsequently be seen in the

---

228 Defixio from Assiut, Upper Egypt, C5th CE, trans. J. Gager.

early (probably eleventh or twelfth century CE) Arabic grimoire, the *Picatrix*.

Sabaoth was another major Hebrew divine name which was popular in the *Greek Magical Papyri*, used in Kabbalah and also found in the books of the Bible.

John Lydus in his sixth century CE work *Liber De Mensibus*, described attributions for these divine names, which whilst they may not be entirely accurate, we may note as being far closer to the time of the original texts and thus worth studying as appropriate contextual meanings:

> "The Chaldeans call the God (Dionysus or Bacchus) Iao in the Phœnician tongue (instead of the intelligible light), and he is often called Sabaoth, signifying that he is above the seven poles, that is the Demiurgus."[229]

These divine names also all occurred in another charm with Hekate, the *Love Spell of attraction performed with the help of heroes or gladiators or those who have died a violent death* (PGM IV.1390-1495).

The divine name of IAO Sabaoth is found in combination with Hekate on an amulet bearing her image and the words *"IAO Sabaoth protect"*.[230] Bonner in his *Studies in Magical Amulets chiefly Greco-Egyptian* also cited an amulet with a triple Hekate on bearing the words IAO Sabaoth Adonai ChO. The last word combined the Greek letters Chi and Omega, which probably represented Jesus, as ChiRo was used as a depiction of Jesus, and Omega as the last letter represented the Christian God. Goodenough in his work *Jewish Symbols in the Greco-Roman Period* also

---

229 Liber De Mensibus, John Lydus, C6th CE, trans. Taylor.
230 Jewish Symbols in the Greco-Roman Period, Vol 2, Goodenough, 1953.

cited other examples of the combination of Hekate with Jewish divine names, showing this was not an infrequent occurrence.

A bronze triple Hekate amulet showing her bearing torches, daggers and scourges with King Solomon on the obverse side performing *hygromanteia* (demon summoning) found at Ostia in Italy, also emphasised the cross-over of Jewish and Greek magic. This connection between Solomon and Greek magic is further indicated in the *Greek Magical Papyri*, where his name was used for three charms against the scorpion of Artemis.[231] The scorpion was connected with Artemis through references such as that of the second century CE Christian theologian Tatian the Assyrian, who wrote *"and the Scorpion the helper of Artemis."*[232]

AMULET SHOWING SOLOMON (LEFT) AND HEKATE (RIGHT)

The name was given as a variant of Solomon, being Salaman, and the same Hebrew divine names were

---

231 PGM XXVIIIa.1-7, PGM XXVIIIb.1-9, PGM XXVIIIc.1-11.
232 Address to the Greeks, Tatian, C2nd CE, trans. J.E. Ryland.

used as seen in the other cross-over charms, i.e. Adonai and Sabaoth. This charm below is typical of the three:

> "Or Or Phor Phor Iao Adaonaei Sabaoth Salaman Tarchchei, I bind you, scorpion of Artemisos, on the 13th."[233]

The combination of Hekate titles and names with the divine names Adonai and Sabaoth as well as numerous Hebrew-derived angelic and divine names occurred in PGM CXXIII.a-f. An unusual element in this magico-medico collection was the phrase *"Come out of your tomb, Christ is calling you"*[234] in the childbearing charm.

Another place where we see a cross-over between Jewish magic and Greek magic connected to Hekate is in the second century Jewish magical text, the *Testament of Solomon*. The *Testament of Solomon* was the first proto-grimoire, giving a catalogue of demons with their controlling angels.

In the *Testament of Solomon* the third and fourth Ephesian Letters, *Lix Tetrax*, were used as the name of a wind demon:

> "But [the demon] answered me: 'I am the spirit of the ashes (Tephras or Lix Tetrax).' And I said to him: 'What is thy pursuit?' And he said: 'I bring darkness on men, and set fire to fields; and I bring homesteads to naught. But most busy am I in summer. However, when I get an opportunity, I creep into corners of the wall, by night and day. For I am offspring of the great one, and nothing less.' Accordingly I said to him: 'Under what star dost thou lie?' And he answered: 'In the very tip of the moon's horn, when it is found in the south. There is my star ... So I

---

233 PGM XXVIIIb.1-9, trans. R. Kotansky.
234 PGM CXXIII.a.50, trans. R. Kotansky.

questioned him, and said: 'And by what name?' And he answered: 'That of the archangel Azael.'"[235]

Additionally there was also reference in the *Testament of Solomon* to the *'bonds of Artemis'* in connection with an unnamed demon, the last of a group of seven female spirits who may have corresponded to the star system of the Pleiades. As the demon said she brought darkness, we can speculate she would have corresponded to the sister called Celaeno, whose name meant *black* or *dark.*

The syncretisation of Hekate and Artemis make this connection an interesting one when exploring the cross-over of Greek and Jewish magic. As Orion was a companion of Artemis who chased the Pleiades for seven years, the biblical reference in the *Book of Job* connecting the Pleiades and bands/bonds does suggest a connection for this verse in the *Testament of Solomon*:

> *"Canst thou bind the sweet influences of Pleiades, or loose the bands of Orion?"*[236]

Significantly this spirit's threat was the one out of all those made by the demons which was achieved. For the reference to the locus referred to the subsequent sacrifice of five locusts to Moloch committed by Solomon to gain the sexual favours of the Queen of Sheba, resulting in the loss of his powers:

> *"Likewise also the seventh said: 'I am the worst, and I make thee worse off than thou wast; because I will impose the bonds of Artemis. But the locust will set me free, for by means thereof is it fated that thou*

---

235 Testament of Solomon 33, c2nd CE, trans. F.C. Conybeare.
236 Job 38:31.

shalt achieve my desire <... > For if one were wise,
he would not turn his steps toward me.'"237

Another connection between Hekate and Solomon may be found through the mandrake plant. Mandrake was sacred to Hekate, and was also used in the demon-expelling ring of Solomon, described by the Jewish historian Flavius Josephus in the first century CE.238

---

237 Testament of Solomon 41, c2nd CE, trans. F.C. Conybeare.
238 Jewish Antiquities, Flavius Josephus, C1st CE, trans. W. Whiston.

CHAPTER 30

FUSIONS

A number of goddesses were partially or fully conflated with Hekate. These were Brimo, Despoina, Enodia, Genetyllis, Kotys, Kratais and Kourotrophos. She was also syncretised with or equated to Artemis, Selene, Mene, Persephone, Physis, Bendis, Bona Dea, Diana, Ereschigal and Isis.

We have concentrated on those goddesses where the syncretisation with Hekate significantly affected perception of her. Specifically these are the goddesses Artemis, Bendis, Bona Dea, Brimo, Despoina, Ereschigal, Isis, Physis and Selene.

Artemis-Hekate

Artemis and Hekate were linked through most of their relationship, an unsurprising fact for such close cousins (their mothers Leto and Asteria were sisters). As well as sharing titles like *Eileithyia*, *Enodia*, *Phosphorus* and *Soteira*, their names were linked as Artemis-Hekate from an early age, as may be seen from this fifth century BCE quote from Aeschylus:

> *"We pray; and that Artemis-Hekate watch over the childbed of their women."*[239]

---

239 Suppliants, Aeschylus; C5th BCE, trans. W. Smyth.

The tendency to portray Artemis with a torch which occurred around this time also resulted in images in sculpture and on vases being more ambiguous, particularly as both goddesses were pictured with dogs and dressed in a similar manner. The result of this has been a number of uncertain images being identified as either or both Hekate and Artemis. When both goddesses were present this was easier, such as in the depiction on the Pergamon Frieze (second century BCE) of Hekate and Artemis together battling giants.

Pliny mentioned in his classic work *Natural History* that there was a statue of Hekate in the precinct of the temple of Artemis at Ephesus,[240] further reinforcing the emphasis of this connection.

Bendis

Bendis was a Thracian moon goddess, who was identified with both Hekate and Artemis. She was first mentioned in literature in the sixth century BCE by the Greek satirical poet Hipponax. He named Bendis as a Thracian goddess along with Cybele.[241] She was also mentioned by the fifth century Athenian comic poet Cratinus in his lost play *The Thracian Women*. A fragment of the play referred to Bendis as being '*two-speared*'.[242]

Farnell in his classic five volume work *The Cults of the Greek States*, wrote:

---

240 Natural History 36.4.32, Pliny, C1st CE.
241 Fragment 127, Hipponax, C6th BCE.
242 Fragment 85, The Thracian Women, Cratinus, 442 BCE.

"We find the undoubtedly Thracian goddess Bendis with many points of likeness to Hekate. The epithet Dilongchos (two-fold) that belonged to the former is explained by Hesychius as describing the goddess who, like Hekate, had power in more than one sphere of nature; and the torch seems to have been the special symbol of both."[243]

Bona Dea

The Roman virgin goddess Bona Dea (*'good goddess'*) was identified with Hekate by the early fifth century CE Neo-Platonist philosopher Macrobius in his work *Saturnalia*. Bona Dea was associated with herbalism (*pharmakeia*) through her attribution of healing goddess, and the serpent was her cult animal, another association she shared with Hekate:

"Others again hold the view that she is Hecate of the Netherworld."[244]

Brimo

Brimo was a Thessalian goddess who became assimilated into Hekate by the fifth century BCE. She was linked with Hekate, Artemis and Selene on defixiones, with Cybele, and she was also associated with Demeter and Persephone in the Orphic funeral tablets, showing a connection between the three Eleusinian goddesses. Brimo was used as a password in the Orphic Mysteries, being recorded on funerary tablets as one of the words the dead soul had to repeat

---

243 The Cults of the Greek States 2:507, Farnell, 1896-1909.
244 Saturnalia, Macrobius, C5th CE, trans. Brouwer.

to prove it was an initiate and entitled to enter the paradisiacal Elysian Fields.[245]

Despoina

Despoina (*the mistress* or *Lady*) was the daughter of Demeter by Poseidon, who covered her as a stallion when she was a mare. The name was also used for both Hekate and Artemis, as seen from surviving fragments by the Greek playwright Aeschylus, with Hekate being called,

"Lady (Despoina) Hekate, before the portal of the royal halls."[246] We may note that this title also emphasised her role as Propylaia.

Ereschigal-Hekate

Ereschigal was the Babylonian chthonian goddess who ruled the underworld. Ereschigal was connected with Hekate both in the *Greek Magical Papyri* and on defixiones. The obvious compatibility of the two chthonian goddesses led to an inevitable syncretisation of Hekate and Ereschigal, as will be seen in the many references in this work.

Ereschigal was also referred to by the title of *Aktiophis* in the *Greek Magical Papyri*. This name occurred four times, particularly in association with Hekate and Selene.

---

245 Pherae tablet 27, C4th BCE.
246 Fragment 216, Aeschylus, c5th BCE, trans. Weir Smith.

Isis-Hekate

Apuleius named Hekate in his *Metamorphoses* (better known as *'The Golden Ass'*) in the late second century CE as one of the many goddesses who were guises of Isis, *"to others Bellona and Hecate and Rhamnusia"*,[247] though as we will show there was more to this than simply the inclusion of another goddess name.

The combination of Hekate and Isis is one which has hitherto been ignored, but one which is clearly illustrated by the images of Isis-Hekate which are depicted on a number of Egyptian coins. Isis-Hekate is pictured on them as triple-faced, with the solar horns and disk found on later images of Isis, which she acquired from the cow-headed goddess Hathor. Additionally Isis-Hekate is depicted facing the Apis bull to the left. That Hekate was also depicted as cow-headed and with numerous bull references associated with her is surely no coincidence.

The other noteworthy points regarding these images are the inclusion of the uraeus serpent in her right hand. Other Greek and Roman images also showed Hekate with a serpent in her hand, although not the cobra which was the uraeus. One image showed a genius flying with crown which it is bringing to Isis-Hekate's head.

Isis-Hekate was also depicted on engraved gems, as seen from a gem showing her in triple form holding serpents, swords and torches.[248] A similar gem is

---

247 Metamorphoses, Apuleus, C2nd CE
248 Catalogue of the Collection of Antique Gems formed by James, ninth earl of Southesk, 1908.

described in the Newell Collection by Bonner in his classic work *Studies in Magical Amulets chiefly Greco-Egyptian.*In the second century CE document Papyrus Oxyrynchus 1380, it was recorded that Isis *"was called Hekate in Caria"*[249] and also *"Artemis of three-fold nature"*,[250] which hinted at the use of Artemis' name to describe Hekate, as frequently happened due to their syncretisation.

An inscription from Kamiros on the Greek island of Rhodes dedicated to Hekate and Serapis by a person who had escaped great danger, indicated that in places the syncretisation of Hekate and Isis was complete.[251]

Physis

Physis should be mentioned, as she was a goddess who seemed to be derived from Hekate, representing a lower aspect of her:

> *"Boundless Physis is suspended from the back of the goddess [Hekate]."*[252]

According to the *Chaldean Oracles*, Physis both represented the moon, and also the functioning of the material world, which the theurgists sought to rise above. So she was not actually evil, although she was associated with earthly daimones who were considered to be deceptive. Theurgists were advised by the *Chaldean Oracles* to avoid Physis:

> *"Do not invoke the self-manifesting image of Physis! Do not look at Physis! For her name is like Fate!"*[253]

---

249 Papyrus Oxyrynchus XI.1380, C2nd CE.
250 Papyrus Oxyrynchus XI.1380, C2nd CE.
251 IG (Inscriptiones Graecae) XII.1.742, date unknown.
252 Chaldean Oracles, C2nd CE, trans. Johnston.
253 Chaldean Oracles, C2nd CE, trans. Johnston.

Physis was described by the early fifth century Greek bishop Synesius as the mother of daimones.[254] In this he was simply drawing on the *Chaldean Oracles*, which stated:

> *"Physis persuades us to believe that the daemones are pure, and that the products of evil matter are propitious and good."*[255]

Selene-Hekate

When the twelfth century Byzantine poet John Tzetzes identified Selene, Artemis and Hekate as the three forms of Hekate,[256] he was continuing an ancient Greek tradition. Hekate-Selene was the most prominent goddess in the *Greek Magical Papyri*, balancing the solar Apollo-Helios as the most prominent god.

The first literary reference to Hekate being lunar occurred in the Roman philosopher Seneca's play Medea, in the first century CE:

> *"I see Trivia's swift gliding car, not as when, radiant, with full face, she drives the livelong night."*[257]

However the earliest possible (though speculative) reference to Artemis as being lunar dated to the third century BCE, in the Greek poet Callimachus' *Hymn 3 to Artemis*, with the silver bow, which could be taken as symbolising the lunar crescent:

> *"And how many times, Goddess, did you test your silver bow?"*[258]

---

254 Hymn 5, Synesius, C5th CE.
255 Chaldean Oracles, C2nd CE, trans. Johnston.
256 Scholiast on Alexandria of Lycophron, C12th CE.
257 Medea, Seneca, C1st CE, trans. Miller.
258 Hymn 3 to Artemis, Callimachus, C3rd BCE, trans. F.J. Nisetich

By the second century BCE the references to Artemis as a lunar goddess were more substantial,[259] and as she had already been associated with Hekate since the fifth century BCE, it is tempting to postulate an earlier lunar association with Selene for Hekate than the first century CE.

'Ω

---

259 E.g. in fragments of the writings of the Stoic philosophers Apollodorus and Diogenes.

BIBLIOGRAPHY

Alexander, Philip S.; *Sepher ha-Razim and the Problem of Black Magic in Early Judaism*; 2003; in *Magic in the Biblical World*, p170-90

Ankarloo, Bengt, & Clark, Stuart (eds); *Witchcraft and Magic in Europe: Vol 2 Ancient Greece and Rome*; 1999; Athlone Press; London

Antoniadi, E.M.; *On Ancient Meteorites, and on the Origin of the Crescent and Star Emblem*; 1939; in *The Journal of the Royal Astronomical Society of Canada* Vol. 33.5:177-84

Apuleius & Griffiths, John Gwyn (trans); *The Isis-book*; 1975; Brill; Leiden

Arnold, Clinton E.; *The Colossian Syncretism*; 1995; Mohr Siebeck; Tubingen

----------; *Ephesians, Power and Magic*; 1989; CUP Archive

Arthur, Rosemary A.; *Ps-Dionysus' Angelic Hierarchy and the Chaldean Oracles*; 2006; in *Studia Patristica* XLII:23-28

Asirvatham, Sulochana Ruth, & Pache, Corinne Ondine, & Watrous, John (eds); *Between Magic and Religion: Interdisciplinary Studies in Ancient Mediterranean Religion and Society*; 2001; Rowan & Littlefield; New York

Athanassakis, Apostolos N. (trans) & Homer; *The Homeric Hymns*; 2004; John Hopkins University Press, Maryland

Athanassiadi, Polymnia, & Frede, Michael (eds); *Pagan Monotheism in Late Antiquity*; 1999; Clarendon Press; Oxford

Audollent, Auguste; *Defixionum Tabellae*; 1967; Minerva; Frankfurt

Aune, David Edward; *Apocalypticism, Prophecy and Magic in Early Christianity*; 2006; Mohr Siebeck; Tubingen

Babbitt, Frank Cole; *Plutarch: Roman Questions*; 1936; William Heinemann Ltd; London

Beale, Gregory K.; *The Book of Revelation: A Commentary on the Greek Text*; 1999; Eerdmans Publishing; Grand Rapids

Berg, William; *Hecate: Greek or 'Anatolian'?*; 1974 in *Numen* Vol 21.2:128-40

Betz, Hans Dieter (ed); *The Greek Magical Papyri in Translation*; 1992; University of Chicago Press; Chicago

----------; *Hellenismus und Urchristentum*; 1990; Mohr Siebeck; Tubingen

Betz, Hans Dieter, & Collins, Adela Yarbro, & Mitchell, Margaret Mary (eds); *Antiquity and Humanity: Essays on Ancient Religion and Philosophy*; 2001; Mohr Siebeck; Tubingen

Blakely, Sandra; *Myth, Ritual, and Metallurgy in Ancient Greece and Recent Africa*; 2006; Cambridge University Press; Cambridge

Bonner, C.; *Studies in Magical Amulets chiefly Greco-Egyptian*; 1950; Ann Arbor; Michigan

Boustan, Ra'anan S., & Reed, Annette Yoshiko (eds); *Heavenly Realms and Earthly Realities in Late Antique Religions*; 2004; Cambridge University Press; Cambridge

Boxall, Ian; *The Revelation of St John*; 2006; Continuum International Publishing Group; London

Bremmer, Jan N., & Veestra, Jan R.; *The Metamorphosis of Magic from Late Antiquity to the Early Modern Period*; 2002; Peeters Publishers; Holland

Brouwer, Hendrik H.J.; *Bona Dea: The Sources and a Description of the Cult*; 1989; Brill; Leiden

Butler, Samuel; *The Odyssey*; 1944; Walter J Black; London

Bryce, A.H., & Campbell, Hugh; *The Seven Books of Arnobius Adversus Gentes*; 1880; T & T Clark; Edinburgh

Celoria, Francis (ed, trans); *The Metamorphoses of Antoninus Liberalis: A Translation With Commentary*; 1992; Routledge; London

Chapman, David W.; *Ancient Jewish and Christian Perceptions of Crucifixion*; 2008; Mohr Siebeck; Tubingen

Clarysse, W., & Schoors, A., & Quaegebeur, J., & Willems, H. (eds); *Egyptian Religion: the Last Thousand Years*; 1998; Peeters; Leuven

Clauss, James J., & Johnston, Sarah Iles (ed); *Medea*; 1997; Princeton University Press; New Jersey

Clauss, Manfred; *The Roman Cult of Mithras: The God and His Mysteries*; 2000; Edinburgh University Press; Edinburgh

Cole, Susan Guettel; *Theoi Megaloi: the Cult of the Great Gods at Samothrace*; 1984; Brill; Leiden

Collins, Derek; *Magic in the Ancient Greek World*; 2008; Blackwell Publishing; Oxford

Conybeare, F.C.; *Philostratus: The Life of Apollonius of Tyana*; 2005; William Heinemann Ltd; London

-----------; *The Testament of Solomon*; 1898; in *Jewish Quarterly Review*, October 1898

Cormack, J.M.R.; *A Tabella Defixionis in the Museum of the University of Reading*; 1951; in HTR 44:25-34

Cory, I.P. (ed); *Ancient Fragments*; 1828; Pickering; London

Cosmopoulos, Michael B.; *Greek Mysteries: The Archaeology and Ritual of Ancient Greek Secret Cults*; 2003; Routledge; London

Damaskios; *Damascii Successoris*; 1966; A.M. Hakkert; Amsterdam

Daniel, Robert W., & Maltomini, Franco (eds, trans); *Supplementum Magicum*; 1990; Westdeutscher Verlag; Opladen

Des Places, E.; *Les Oracles Chaldaïques*; 1984; in ANRW 17.4:2299-2335

D'Este, Sorita; *Triple Horns of the Greek Magical Papyri*; 2008; in *Horns of Power*; p189-94; Avalonia; London

Dickie, Matthew; *Magic and Magicians in the Greco-Roman World*; 2003; Routledge; London

Dickinson, Oliver T.P.K.; *The Aegean Bronze Age*; 1994; Cambridge University Press; Cambridge

Dillon, Matthew; *Girls and Women in Classical Greek Religion*; 2003; Routledge; London

----------; *Pilgrims and Pilgrimage in Ancient Greece*; 1997; Routledge; London

Duff, J.D. (trans): *Lucan: Pharsalia*; 1942; William Heinemann Ltd; London

Edmonds III, Prof. Radcliffe G.; *Ephesia Grammata*; 2009; www.brynmawr.edu/classics/redmonds/H5-CSTS212.html

Edwards, Charles M.; *The Running Maiden from Eleusis and the Early Classical Image of Hekate*; 1986; in *American Journal of Archaeology* 90.3:307-318

Evelyn-White, Hugh G.; *Hesiod: The Homeric Hymns and Homerica*; 1941; William Heinemann Ltd; London

Faraone, Christopher A.; *Ancient Greek Love Magic*; 1999; Harvard University Press; Massachusetts

Faraone, Christopher A., & Obbink, Dirk; *Magika Hiera: Ancient Greek Magic & Religion*; 1991; Oxford University Press; Oxford

Farnell, Lewis Richard; *The Cults of the Greek States* (5 volumes); 1896; Clarendon Press; Oxford

Felton, D.; *Haunted Greece and Rome*; 19991 University of Texas Press; Texas

Fletcher, William (trans); *The Divine Institutes of Lactantius*; 1886; in *Ante-Nicene Fathers* Vol 7; Christian Literature Publishing Co; New York

Fowler, H.W. & F.G. (trans); *The Works of Lucian of Samosata*; 1905; The Clarendon Press; Oxford

Frazer, J.G. (trans); *Pausanias's Description of Greece*; 1898; The MacMillan Company; New York

Fullerton, Mark D.; *The Archaistic Style in Roman Statuary*; 1990; Brill; Leiden

Gager, John R.; *Curse Tablets and Binding Spells from the Ancient World*; 1992; Oxford University Press; Oxford

Gifford, E.H. (trans); *Eusebius of Caesarea: Praeparatio Evangelica*; 1903; Horatio Hart; London

Goldin, Owen, & Kilroe, Patricia; *Human Life and the Natural World: Readings in the History of Western Philosophy*; 1997; Broadview Press Ltd; Canada

Goodenough, E.R.; *Jewish Symbols in the Greco-Roman Period*; 1992; Princeton University Press; Princeton

Graf, Fritz; *Magic in the Ancient World*; 1997; Harvard University Press; Massachusetts

----------; *What is new about Greek sacrifice?*; 2002; in *Kykeon: studies in honour of H.S. Versnel*; p113-26; Brill; Leiden

Graf, Fritz, & Johnston, Sarah Iles; *Ritual Texts for the Afterlife: Orpheus and the Bacchic Gold Tablets*; 2007; Routledge; London

Gregory, Horace (trans); *The Metamorphoses by Ovid*; 2001; Signet Classics

Guthrie, W.K.C.; *Orpheus and Greek Religion: A Study of the Orphic Movement*; 1993; Princeton University Press; Princeton

Hall, Jonathan M.; *Ethnic Identity in Greek Antiquity*; 2000; Cambridge University Press; Cambridge

Harmon, A.M. (trans); *Lucian* (8 volumes); 1936; William Heinemann; London

Head, Barclay V.; *A Catalogue of the Greek Coins in the British Museum*; 1906; Woodfall and Kinder; London

Hermann, Gottfried (trans); *Orphica*; 1805; Leipzig

Hornblower, Simon, & Matthews, Elaine; *Greek Personal Names: Their Value as Evidence*; 2000; Oxford University Press; Oxford

Hueffer, Oliver Madox; *The Book of Witches*; 1908; Eveleigh Nash; London

Isaac, Benjamin H.; *The Greek Settlements in Thrace Until the Macedonian Conquest*; 1986; Brill; Leiden

Jebb, Richard Claverhouse (trans); *The Characters of Theophrastus*; 1870; Macmillan; London

Johnston, Sarah Iles; *Hekate Soteira*; 1990; Scholars Press; Atlanta

----------; *Restless Dead: Encounters between the Living and the Dead in Ancient Greece*; 1999; University of California Press; California

Johnson, W.R.; *Momentary Monsters: Lucan and his Heroes*; 1987; Cornell University Press

Kaibel, Georg; *Comicorum Graecorum Fragmenta*; 1958; Apud Weidmannos

Kater-Sibbes, G.J. F., & Vermaseren, Maarten Jozef; *Apis: Inscriptions, Coins and Addenda*; 1977; Brill; Leiden

Kingsley, Peter; *Ancient Philosophy, Mystery, and Magic*; 1995, Clarendon Press; Oxford

Kirk, G.S., & Raven, J.S., & Schofield, M. (eds); *The Presocratic Philosophers: A Critical History with a Selection of Texts*; 1983; Cambridge University Press; Cambridge

Klauck, Hans-Josef & McNeil, Brian; *The Religious Context of Early Christianity: A Guide to Greco-Roman Religions*; 2003; Continuum International Publishing Group; London

Kottek, Samuel S.; *Medicine and Hygiene in the Works of Flavius Josephus*; 1994; Brill; Leiden

Klutz, Todd (ed.); *Magic in the Biblical World: From the Rod of Aaron to the Ring of Solomon*; 2003; T&T Clark International; London

----------; *Rewriting the Testament of Solomon: Tradition, Conflict and Identity in a Late Antique Pseudepigraphon*; 2005; T&T Clark International; London

Kraus, Theodor; *Hekate: Studien zu Wesen u. Bilde der Göttin in Kleinasien u. Griechenland*; 1960; Heidelberg

Larson, Jennifer Lynn; *Greek Nymphs: Myth, Cult, Love*; 2001; Oxford University Press; Oxford

Legge, F.; *Philosophumena or The Refutation of All Heresies, formerly attributed to Origen but now to Hippolytus*; 1921; The MacMillan Company; New York

Lloyd, Geoffrey Ernest Richard; *Science, Folklore, and Ideology: Studies in the Life Sciences in Ancient Greece*; 1983; Cambridge University Press; Cambridge

Luck, Georg; *Arcana Mundi: Magic and the Occult in the Greek and Roman Worlds*; 1985; John Hopkins University Press, Maryland

----------; *Ancient Pathways & Hidden Pursuits: Religion, Magic & Morals in the Ancient World*; 2000; Michigan University Press; Michigan

Luibheld, C. (trans); *Pseudo-Dionysus: The Complete Works*; 1987; New York

Mair, A.W. & G.R. (trans); *Callimachus Hymns and Epigrams. Lycophron. Aratus*; 1921; William Heinemann; London

Marconi, Clemente & Getty Foundation; *Temple Decoration and Cultural Identity in the Archaic Greek World*; 2007; Cambridge University Press; Cambridge

Mead, G.R.S.; *Pistis Sophia*; 1921; John M. Watkins; London

Miller, Frank Justus; *Seneca's Tragedies Volume I: Hercules Furens, Troades, Medea, Hippolytus, Oedipus*; 1960; Harvard University Press; Harvard

Mirecki, Paul Allen, & Meyer, Marvin (eds); *Magic and Ritual in the Ancient World*; 2002; Brill; Leiden

Morgan, M.A. (ed); *Sepher ha-Razim: The Book of Mysteries*; 1983; Chico; California

Naveh, Joseph & Shaked, Saul; *Magic Spells and Formulae: Aramaic Incantations of Late Antiquity*; 1993; Magnes Press; Jerusalem

Nichols, Steve; *Taro of the Four Worlds*; 2006; Steve Nichols

Nisetich, Frank J. (trans); *The Poems of Callimachus*; 2001; Oxford University Press; Oxford

Noegel, Scott B., & Walker, Joel Thomas, & Wheeler, Brannon M. (eds); *Prayer, Magic, and the Stars in the Ancient and Late Antique World*; 2003; Penn State University Press; Pennsylvania

Nordh, Katarina; *Aspects of Ancient Egyptian Curses and Blessings: Conceptual Background and Transmission*; 1996; Uppsala Studies in Ancient Mediterranean and Near Eastern Civilizations; Uppsala

Novak, Ralph Martin; *Christianity and the Roman Empire: Background Texts*; 2001; Continuum International Publishing Group

Ogden, Daniel; *Magic, Witchcraft, and Ghosts in the Greek and Roman Worlds*; 2002; Oxford University Press; Oxford

-----------; *Binding Spells: Curse Tablets and Voodoo Dolls in the Greek and Roman Worlds*; 1999; in *Witchcraft and Magic in Europe Volume 2: Ancient Greece and Rome*; Athlone Press; London

O'Neill, Edward (ed); *Plutarch: Moralia*; 2004; William Heinemann Ltd; London

Parisinou, Eva; *The Light of the Gods: The Role of Light in Archaic and Classical Greek Cult*; 2000; Duckworth; London

Parker, Robert; *Miasma: Pollution and Purification in Early Greek Religion*; 1996; Clarendon Press; Oxford

Petrie, W.M.F.; *Ancient Egypt*; 1915; MacMillan and Co; London

Pinch, Geraldine; *Magic in Ancient Egypt*; 1994; British Museum Press; London

Price, Theodora Hadzisteliou; *Kourotrophos: Cults and Representations of the Greek Nursing Deities*; 1978; Brill; Leiden

Roberts, Rev. Alexander & Donaldson, James (eds); *The Seven Books of Arnobius Adversus Gentes*; 1871; T & T Clark; Edinburgh

Rohde, Erwin; *Psyche: The Cult of Souls and the Belief in Immortality Among the Greeks*; 2000; Routledge; London

Roller, Lynn E.; *In Search of God the Mother: the Cult of Anatolian Cybele*; 1999; University of California Press; California

Ronan, Stephen (ed); *The Goddess Hekate*; 1992; Chthonios Books; Hastings

----------; *Hekate's Iynx: An Ancient Theurgical Tool*; 1991; in Alexandria I:321-335, Grand Rapids

Ross, Charles Stanley (trans); *The Thebaid by Publius Papinius Statius*; 2004; John Hopkins University Press, Maryland

Rouse, W.H.D.; *Nonnus Dionysiaca Books 1-48*; 1960; Harvard University Press; Cambridge

Ryland, J.E. (trans); *Tatian's Address to the Greeks*; 1886; in *Ante-Nicene Fathers* Vol 2; Christian Literature Publishing Co; New York

Schafer, Peter, & Kippenberg, Hans Gerhard (eds); *Envisioning Magic*; 1997; Brill; Leiden

Scholfield, Alwyn Faber (trans); *Aelian: On the Characteristics of Animals*; 1959; Harvard University Press; Harvard

Seaton, R.C. (trans); *Apollonius Rhodius: Argonautica*; 1990; LOEB Classical Library

Shakespeare, William; *Macbeth: A Tragedy in Five Acts*; 1848; M Douglas; New York

Skinner, Stephen & Rankine, David; *The Goetia of Dr Rudd*; 2007; Golden Hoard Press; Singapore

----------- & -----------; *The Veritable Key of Solomon*; 2008; Golden Hoard Press; Singapore

Smith, A.H.; *A Catalogue of Engraved Gems in the British Museum*; 1888; British Museum; London

Smith, K.F.; *Hekate's Suppers*; 1992 in *The Goddess Hekate*; p56-64; Chthonios Books; Hastings

Southesk, James Carnegie, & Carnegie, Lady Helena Mariota; *Catalogue of the Collection of Antique Gems Formed by James, Ninth Earl of Southesk, K.T.*; 1908; B. Quaritch

Strelan, Rick; *Outside are the Dogs and the Sorcerors*; 2003; in *Biblical Theology Bulletin* 33:148-57

Stückenbruck, Loren T.; *Angel Veneration and Christology: A Study in Early Judaism and in the Christology of the Apocalypse of John*; 1995; Mohr Siebeck; Tubingen

Suda online; *www.stoa.org/sol/*

Tavenner, Eugene; *Iynx and Rhombus*; 1933; in *Transactions and Proceedings of the American Philological Association*, Vol. 64:109-127

Taylor, Thomas; *Iamblichus On The Mysteries* (translated from the Greek); 1821; Chiswick

-----------; *Select Works of Porphyry*; 1823; Thomas Rodd; London

Theophrastus; *Enquiry into Plants Books VI-IX*; 1989; Harvard University Press; Cambridge

Torijano, Pablo A.; *Solomon the Esoteric King: From King to Magus, Development of a Tradition*; 2002; Brill; Leiden

Treister, Michail Yu, & Hargrave, James; *Hammering Techniques in Greek and Roman Jewellery and Toreutics*; 2001; Brill; Leiden

Von Jan, Ludwig (ed); *Macrobius: The Saturnalia*; 1852; Gottfried Bass; Quedlingberg & Liepzig

Various; *Plays of the Greek Dramatists: Selections from Aeschylus, Sophocles, Euripides and Aristophanes*; ND; Puritan Publishing Company Inc; Illinois

Vermaseren, Maarten Jozef, & Lane, Eugene; *Cybele, Attis and Related Cults*; 1996; Brill; Leiden

Versnel, H.S., & Horstmanshoff, H.F.J., & Singor, H.W.; *Kykeon: studies in honour of H.S. Versnel*; 2002; Brill; Leiden

Von Rudolf, Robert; *Hekate in Ancient Greek Religion*; 1999; Horned Owl Publishing; Victoria

Walters, Kerry S., & Portmess, Lisa; *Religious Vegetarianism: From Hesiod to the Dalai Lama*; 2001; SUNY Press; New York

West, David R.; *Some Cults of Greek Goddesses and Female Daemons of Oriental Origin*; 1995; Butzon & Bercker; Kevelaer

Whiston, William (trans); *The Works of Josephus*; 1987; Hendrickson

Willoughby, Harold R.; *Pagan Regeneration: A Study of Mystery Initiations in the Greco-Roman World*; 1929; University of Chicago Press; Chicago

Wunsch, R (ed); *De Mensibus*; 1898; Teuber; Leipzig

Xenophon; *Xenophon in Seven Volumes*; 1979; Harvard University Press; Cambridge

Young, F., Edwards, M., & Parvis, P. (eds); *Studia Patristica* XLII; 2006; Peeters; Leuven

INDEX

Aigina 19, 25, 92, 93

Amphiphon 128

Amulet 70, 87, 102, 104, 163, 164, 165

Anubis 71, 80

Aphrodisias.................. 21

Aphrodite 72, 73, 78, 82, 104, 159

Apollo 25, 27, 28, 29, 57, 73, 175

Ares 24

Argos 19, 25

Aristaios 26, 27

Artemis 23, 25, 28, 49, 50, 53, 59, 60, 68, 70, 72, 73, 75, 79, 82, 88, 98, 134, 136, 139, 155, 165, 167, 169, 170, 171, 172, 174, 175, 176

Astarte 23

Asteria 25, 26, 27, 114, 169

Athena 50, 100, 121

Athens 22, 29, 59, 87, 157

Atropos 133, 136

Attica 21, 48, 162

Attis 28

Babylon 147, 160

Bacchic Gold Funeral Tablets 32, 54

Bactria 111

Baubo 53, 75, 88

Bendis 28, 155, 169, 170, 171

Black Dog 91, 114, 124, 154, 155

Bona Dea 28, 169, 171

Brimo 26, 28, 55, 58, 66, 75, 77, 98, 101, 155, 163, 169, 171

Bull 41, 62, 119, 134, 137, 138, 173

Byzantium.................. 112

Canidia................. 45, 145

Caria 20, 21, 22, 174

Cerberus 95, 98, 135, 148, 152, 153

Ceres........................... 28

Chthonia 20, 28, 86, 87, 95, 114, 130, 145, 151

Circe 29, 30, 37, 41, 42, 82, 94, 95, 99, 101, 143

Claudiopolis 53

Clotho 133, 136

Colchis 45

Cow 71, 80, 137, 173

Crete...................... 66, 73

Cronos................. 92, 134

Crossroads 59, 60, 72, 76, 81, 82, 96, 97, 124, 126, 128, 154

Cybele 20, 23, 27, 28, 58, 110, 116, 170, 171

Dactyls 77, 91

Dadouchos............. 20, 56

Daimones 60, 67, 78, 86, 116, 120, 121, 145, 153, 174, 175

Defixiones 28, 53, 71, 84, 85, 86, 87, 88, 102, 105, 141, 151, 157, 163, 171, 172

Delos 25

Demeter 23, 24, 26, 27, 28, 39, 44, 48, 49, 50, 51, 52, 53, 54, 55, 56, 61, 151, 171, 172

Deo .... See Demeter

Despoina...... 28, 169, 172

Diana............. 28, 60, 169

Dionysus...27, 43, 53, 164

Diwija 23

Dog 24, 41, 59, 62, 71, 72, 73, 74, 79, 81, 96, 97, 106, 110, 123, 124, 135, 137, 139, 140, 141, 152, 153, 154, 155, 156

Dragon 105, 137, 139, 152

Dream Oracle 114

Dreams 25, 72, 114, 115, 116, 155

Egypt 73, 96, 106, 147, 162, 163

Eileithyia 119, 169

Eleusis 19, 24, 28, 45, 48, 49, 50, 53, 54, 55, 56, 60, 91

Elysian Fields20, 151, 172

Empedocles 32, 37, 38, 39, 46, 103, 147

Enodia 20, 28, 60, 66, 169

Ephesian Letters 65, 66, 67, 73, 75, 76, 91, 166

Ereschigal 28, 53, 70, 71, 72, 73, 76, 88, 169, 172

Erictho44, 45, 143, 145, 146, 147

Fates 133, 136

Ge 27, 28, 50, 84, 86

Genetyllis 28, 155, 156, 169

Ghost 42, 60, 63, 78, 79, 80, 84, 86, 114, 115, 120, 121, 122, 126, 131, 144, 145

Goat 72, 80, 106, 135, 137, 139, 140

Hades 28, 44, 50, 51, 82, 83, 84, 86, 135, 147, 149, 151, 152, 155

Hekabe 154, 155

Hekataion 21, 59

Hekate Suppers 120, 124, 126, 127

Hekatesia 22

Helios 28, 29, 30, 50, 52, 78, 110, 133, 175

Hercules 95, 152, 184

Hermekate 29, 71

Hermes 27, 28, 29, 41, 47, 51, 61, 71, 72, 78, 80, 84, 86, 87, 95, 106, 114, 122, 151

Hesiod 22, 23, 25, 37, 38, 46, 68, 87, 102, 152

Honey 27, 46, 114, 122, 123, 144, 152

Horse 62, 137, 140, 141

Inanna 20, 23

Iphigenia 23, 68

Iphimedeia 23

Iris 51

Isis 28, 54, 71, 169, 173, 174

Iynges 108

Iynx 82, 83, 104, 159, 160, 161

Janus 132, 133

Jason 39, 42, 43, 90, 97, 100, 101, 121, 123, 149, 157, 159

Jesus 40, 107, 117, 118, 164

Kamiros 174

Keres 149

Kleidouchos 20, 151

Kore .... See Persephone

Kotys 28, 169

Kourotrophos 20, 28, 78, 169

Kratais 28, 30, 169

Kykeon 51, 53, 55, 56

Lachesis 133, 136

Lagina .. 18, 20, 21, 24, 53

Lampads 45

Leto 25, 169

Linear B tablet Tn316 ... 23

Lion 24, 110, 112, 118

Medea 29, 30, 37, 39, 41, 42, 43, 44, 45, 82, 90, 94, 95, 97, 99, 100, 101, 117, 120, 121, 123, 139, 146, 147, 149, 159

Mene 28, 64, 71, 72, 134, 136, 169

Miletus 21

Mithras 27, 28

Mount Etna 39, 103

Nails 84, 102, 105

Necromancy 41, 121, 143, 144, 145, 146, 147, 148

Nexichthon 75, 151

Nightmares 114

Nike 58, 73

Nysa 50, 53

Nyx 26, 27, 73, 151

Odysseus 41, 144, 154, 155

Olympus 29, 51, 134, 151, 159

Orpheus....54, 58, 92, 123

Osiris 71, 88

Ostia 70, 87, 102, 104, 165

Ouranos 27

Pamphylia 110

Patera 103, 110

Paulina 28

Pausanias 29

Pegasus 111

Pereswa 23

Pergamon Frieze 59, 155, 170

Persephone 23, 24, 27, 28, 29, 39, 44, 48, 49, 50, 51, 52, 53, 54, 55, 56, 60, 65, 70, 71, 72, 73, 79, 84, 86, 133, 134, 136, 152, 169, 171

Perses 25, 29, 30, 38, 41, 123

Persia 147

Phalasarna 66, 73

Pharmakeia 37, 44, 55, 94, 171

Pherae 112, 172

Phosphorus 20, 56, 116, 145, 169

Phrygia 20

Physis .. 28, 169, 174, 175

Pleiades 167

Pluto 71, 80, 87

Porphyry 34, 37, 39, 40, 41, 47, 61, 62, 64, 68, 103, 116, 117, 118, 119, 122, 136, 153

Poseidon 49, 112, 172

Propolos 20, 51, 56, 86

Propylaia 20, 21, 29, 49, 60, 172

Prytania 149

Purphoros 56

Pylos 23

Restless Dead 85, 96, 143, 150, 153

Rhea 28, 91

Rhizotomoi 37

Rhodes 174

Samothrace 19, 25, 54, 92

Scylla 30

Selene 24, 28, 60, 70, 72, 73, 78, 79, 80, 81, 108, 133, 134, 136, 137, 139, 140, 141, 169, 171, 172, 175, 176

Selinus 19, 24, 39, 54

Serapis 174

Serpent 62, 76, 98, 135, 137, 141, 142, 158, 171, 173

Sicily.......... 19, 24, 39, 54

Skylakagetis................. 30

Sobek........................... 81

Solomon 70, 87, 97, 102, 104, 163, 165, 167, 168

Soteira 20, 169

Strophalos 108, 159, 160, 161

Stylus 80, 85, 102

Synocheis 108

Talos.......................... 149

Teletarchai................. 108

Thera 43, 116

Thessaly 37, 39, 44, 45, 112, 141, 143, 147

Theurgy........................41

Thoth 73

Thrace............ 22, 92, 155

Torches 49, 52, 56, 57, 60, 61, 66, 70, 87, 98, 110, 111, 112, 128, 155, 157, 158, 165, 173

Triformis 20, 93, 110, 111

Trimorphos.....26, 60, 155

Trioditis............20, 60, 87

Trivia...... 59, 60, 129, 175

Voces Magicae 65, 66, 67, 68, 69, 71, 72, 76, 77, 80, 88, 136, 153, 163

Zeus 25, 26, 27, 28, 38, 42, 50, 51, 71, 73, 91, 97, 111, 119, 132, 133, 135

LaVergne, TN USA
28 November 2010
206550LV00001B/7/P